Everyday

SUN

magic

About the Author

Dorothy Morrison is a Wiccan High Priestess of the Georgian Tradition. She founded the Coven of the Crystal Garden in 1986. An avid practitioner of the Ancient Arts for more than twenty years, she spent many years teaching the Craft to students throughout the United States and Australia, and is a member of the Pagan Poets Society.

To Write to the Author

If you wish to contact the author or would like more information about this book, please write to the author in care of Llewellyn Worldwide and we will forward your request. Both the author and publisher appreciate hearing from you and learning of your enjoyment of this book and how it has helped you. Llewellyn Worldwide cannot guarantee that every letter written to the author can be answered, but all will be forwarded. Please write to:

Dorothy Morrison
℅ Llewellyn Worldwide
P.O. Box 64383, Dept. 0-7387-0468-7
St. Paul, MN 55164-0383, U.S.A.

Please enclose a self-addressed stamped envelope for reply,
or $1.00 to cover costs. If outside the U.S.A., enclose
an international postal reply coupon.

Many of Llewellyn's authors have websites with additional information and resources. For more information, please visit our website at:

http://www.llewellyn.com

Everyday

SUN

magic

**SPELLS &
RITUALS FOR
RADIANT
LIVING**

DOROTHY MORRISON

Llewellyn Publications
St. Paul, Minnesota

Everyday Sun Magic: Spells & Rituals for Radiant Living © 2005 by Dorothy Morrison. All rights reserved. No part of this book may be used or reproduced in any manner whatsoever, including Internet usage, without written permission from Llewellyn Publications except in the case of brief quotations embodied in critical articles and reviews.

First Edition
First Printing, 2005

Cover design by Kevin R. Brown
Editing and interior design by Karin Simoneau
Sunglasses and plant image © 2004 by PhotoDisc

Library of Congress Cataloging-in-Publication Data
Morrison, Dorothy, 1955–
   Everyday sun magic: spells & rituals for radiant living /
   Dorothy Morrison.
       p.   cm.
   Includes bibliographical references and index.
   ISBN 0-7387-0468-7
     1. Magic. 2. Sun—Miscellanea. I. Title.
   BF1623.S8M67 2005
   133.4'3—dc22   2004057710

Llewellyn Worldwide does not participate in, endorse, or have any authority or responsibility concerning private business transactions between our authors and the public.

All mail addressed to the author is forwarded but the publisher cannot, unless specifically instructed by the author, give out an address or phone number.

Any Internet references contained in this work are current at publication time, but the publisher cannot guarantee that a specific location will continue to be maintained. Please refer to the publisher's website for links to authors' websites and other sources.

Llewellyn Publications
A Division of Llewellyn Worldwide, Ltd.
P.O. Box 64383, Dept. 0-7387-0468-7
St. Paul, MN 55164-0383, U.S.A.
www.llewellyn.com

Printed in the United States of America

Also by Dorothy Morrison

Magical Needlework

Everyday Magic: Spells & Rituals for Modern Living

In Praise of the Crone: A Celebration of Feminine Maturity

The Whimsical Tarot

Yule: A Celebration of Light & Warmth

Bud, Blossom, & Leaf:
The Magical Herb Gardener's Handbook

The Craft: A Witch's Book of Shadows

The Craft Companion

Everyday Tarot Magic

Everyday Moon Magic

Enchantments of the Heart

To the founders of the RavenMyst Circle Tradition—Chris and David Norris, Maggie Shayne, Mary Caliendo, and Nicole Greevy—who truly are ten feet tall and bulletproof.

In memory of . . . Tempest Smith—the Southern Sun—who, in her passing, not only left a legacy of tolerance, but proved that one person's life can make a huge difference in the lives of those left behind.

Contents

Acknowledgments

This book could not have come to be without the help of many people. Some provided guidance, shed light on difficult subjects, and spent countless hours seeking documentation for the more obscure information I'd come across. Others offered advice and kept me on track, insisting that even the most controversial facts be included. And then, there were those who simply reminded me to laugh, to have fun, and yes, even to breathe. Still, there were others whose work behind the scenes was so remarkable that I couldn't possibly let this opportunity pass without a very special thank you!

To my husband, Mark, who lights my world with his smiles, warms my heart with his hugs, and ignites the person I am with his love. You truly are my sunshine—and I love you without measure!

To Murv for his constant friendship and neverending patience during my dry spells—even when my response to his insistence that the Muses would surface was "Yeah, but . . ."

To Mary Anne Weishuhn and Linda Milam for diligent research on Sunday observance. Had it not been for you, I'd have certainly pulled my hair out!

To Mary Caliendo for sharing her extensive knowledge of historical and theological facts, and for graciously allowing the use of her wish runes and entity-banishing ritual.

To Bick Thomas for lending his expertise to the Egyptian aspects of this book, for content suggestions, and for making me laugh when I didn't think I could.

To Jay French for immeasurable help in tracking down the source of the archangel seals, and for graciously offering the use of his versions.

To Karin Simoneau for not only seeing to it that I always look good in print, but for slaying the darkest, most indomitable demons right in the nick of time— even when it's not her job!

To Z. Harrell for listening and commiserating, encouraging, and prodding—and for just being you!

To Lexi Kavanaugh for birthing the newsletter, great publicity, keeping me apprised of where I'm supposed to be and when, handling everything from the important to the ridiculous, and many other things too numerous to mention.

May the Sun always light your way, warm your hearts, and wrap you in the golden magic that only He can boast!

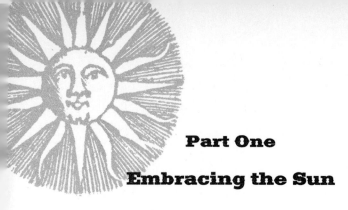

Part One

Embracing the Sun

He ends the night and heralds the day
He wakes us up for work and play
He stirs the seed deep in the Earth
And sends it sprouting through Her girth
He rules our months, our seasons, and days
And with His Fire, He lights our way
He brings us joy and warms our hearts
He promises a brand new start
He doles out doses of Vitamin D
To increase our calcium absorbency
He brings us air and stirs the tides
And all the while, through the sky He rides
Without a cross word or a single objection
Do you know who He is? Have you made the connection?
He is none other than the glorious Sun
Who only finds rest when our day is done

—Dorothy Morrison

1

Good Morning, Sunshine

The Sun is perhaps the most important influence in our lives. He heralds the coming of each new day, and lets us know that it's time to get up and get going. But more importantly, His appearance actually makes us *feel* like getting something done. In His light, we're motivated to move about, grab our to-do lists, and become productive members of humankind—something crucial in today's busy world. No one I know can afford to waste a perfectly good day.

But the very sight of Him does much more for us than that. It just can't help but make us smile. And that even goes for folks like me who aren't morning people at all. There's just something downright joyous about seeing the Sun light the world around us. The Sun lightens our moods, quickens our steps, warms our hearts, and just generally makes us happier people.

Those aren't the only things the Sun does for us, though. He also contributes largely to our good health. How? By supplying our recommended daily dosage of Vitamin D, the very substance that helps the body to absorb calcium.[1] And not only does the Sun manage this without effort on His part, He manages it without effort on ours. Only about ten minutes of sunshine per day does the trick—and we're well on our way to having healthy bones and stronger bodies.

The Sun's list of responsibilities goes on and on. He rules our calendar, starts each week by holding dominion over Sunday, and marks the comings and goings of the seasons in the cycles of His journey. His position in the sky at the time of our births is responsible for our natal signs, and thus He is largely responsible for how the rest of the world views us. He's responsible for the blowing of the winds, the growth of the plants, flowers, and trees that populate the Earth, and for the oxygen we breathe. And even with all this stuff on His plate, He still finds time to entertain us with sunbeams, rainbows, sundogs, and the like. I'd say that He's a very busy star,[2] indeed.

Taking all this into consideration, it's little wonder that the Sun has managed to infiltrate our lives as a household word. We say that happy people have a sunny disposition, and refer to those with freckled faces as being sun-kissed. Florida is known as "The Sunshine State," and Japan and Scandinavia are known as the lands of the "rising sun" and "midnight sun," respectively. We don sunglasses and sun hats, then head for the beach to sunbathe (but not before applying our sunblock; otherwise, we might wind up with a sunburn). We add sun porches to our homes, and have sunroofs installed in our vehicles. But it doesn't stop there. We also brew sun tea, order our eggs sunny-side up, and purchase Sunny Delight at the grocery store.

Even the realm of musical entertainment isn't immune to the influences of that big, blazing, gaseous mass that warms our backs and lights our way. Remember that fun and campy little song you probably sang in kindergarten called "You Are My Sunshine"? Or maybe you remember "Good Morning, Sunshine," "Sunny," and "Here Comes the Sun" if you're from my generation. And what about the film and television industries? *A Place in the Sun,* starring Elizabeth Taylor and Montgomery Clift, is a classic, as is *A Raisin in the Sun,* with Sidney Poitier. And no one could forget John Lithgow's hilarious sitcom *Third Rock from the Sun.*

The Sun influences our lives in other ways, too. If it weren't for the Sun, in fact, life as we know it would simply cease to exist. Without His warming presence, plant life would be nearly nonexistent. Vegetables would be limited to root crops like potatoes and carrots. And flowers? Well, they'd be a thing of the past as well, since even those that bloom at night need His light and warmth to bring them to bud.

But even if we could do without all those amenities, other problems would surface. Without sunlight, electric bills would skyrocket, and without warmth, so would heating bills. And there's no way we could just go back to the basics of firewood and candlelight. Why? Because without the warming rays of the Sun, trees would be in short supply. And using them for heating, cooking, and melting wax would not only drive them to extinction, but would present a much larger problem: a total lack of oxygen to our planet. The Earth would become a cold, dark, dank place. For all practical purposes, it would be virtually uninhabitable.

And yet we tend to take the Sun for granted. We simply expect it to rise each day and light the Earth. Maybe it's not our fault, though. Since we live in such a modernized world, the magic of the Sun seems nothing less than commonplace. But no matter whose fault it is, such an attitude is also pure and unadulterated travesty—for the magic of the Sun is truly nothing less than miraculous!

Who's Got the Time?

Precisely who first revered the Sun's daily comings and goings as more than just a common occurrence is anybody's guess; in fact, it's been the subject of academic and anthropological debate for centuries. Some insist that the Sumerians and/or Babylonians initially used solar cycles to measure time. However, most believe that the ancient Egyptians were the first to refine this use to the point of any sort of predictability.[3] The first clocks weren't the sundials you might expect, though, and they really didn't keep track of minutes or hours. Instead, they were more like a calendar in the form of obelisk-shaped stone structures or buildings. And when the Sun shone upon them, He cast a shadow on the ground that not only measured days, months, and years, but the seasons as well.

But the Egyptians probably weren't the only ones who used the cycle of the Sun for time measurement. Take Stonehenge, for example, which announces and measures the solstices. The rising Sun at Midsummer casts a U-shaped shadow on the stones, and this shadow opens toward the growing light. At Yule, though, the reverse is true. The shape appears again, but only with the setting Sun, and it opens toward the fading light. And while nobody really knows all the intended uses of Stonehenge— some experts think it was originally built as an astronomical observatory, while others insist it was constructed solely as a temple to the Sun—or if it marks or measures other days, one thing's for sure: the only time this phenomenon occurs is at the solstices. And that makes it a safe bet that time measurement was at least one of the reasons for its construction.

Some time around 300 BC, solar time-keeping devices were improved to measure hours. One of the improvements was the creation of a circular arc divided into twelve equal sections with a bead in the center. But since the days varied in length from season to season, so did the hours. And because these time measurements weren't very accurate, they came to be known as *temporary hours*. It wasn't until the Greeks discovered the use of angles and gave birth to geometry and trigonometry that things began to improve. Even with all of that, though, it took another thousand years to figure out how to determine the *equal hours*[4] we know today.

But what about the calendar? How on earth did we wind up with a solar calendar when we know that ancient civilizations initially marked time by the cycles of the Moon? Well, while the Moon definitely came and went with regularity, She just didn't mark the seasons accurately. And this was an awful problem for the early peoples since they were agricultural in nature. There was no way to know when to plant or when to harvest. This was especially problematic for the ancient Egyptians, though, for an accurate forecast of the seasons also provided an accurate prediction of the flooding of the Nile River. And without knowledge of the latter, the crops that fed and clothed the civilized world might simply be washed away.

So realizing that the Sun—rather than the Moon—announced the change of the seasons, the Egyptians made some changes around 4000 BC. They added five days to their twelve month, 360-day calendar to align it to the Sun's cycles. In doing so, though, they forgot about the fourth of a day left over, and that was a terrible mistake. Why? Because after years and years, that quarter day added up, and pretty soon, the months they'd marked as Summer were coming in the Winter. The seasons were completely out of sync, and they had a bigger mess on their hands than they'd ever had at the outset.

Finally, around 45 BC, Julius Caesar made some changes. He decreed that the first year be 455 days in length to bring the seasons back to order. Then he based the new calendar on the solar year at 365¼ days. And to catch up with the accumulation of those quarter days, he instituted a leap year that fell every four years. It was a good plan, but it was still a little more than eleven minutes off per year, and even though that doesn't seem like much, there was still enough of a discrepancy to cause a problem. Enough so, in fact, that by the fifteenth century, things were off by about a week.

It wasn't until the sixteenth century that the solar calendar was straightened out by Pope Gregory XIII, who incorporated some mathematical formulas to remove three leap years every four hundred years. This Gregorian calendar—the calendar we use today—is fairly accurate, but still not perfect. Not to worry, though. At this point, we're only about twenty-six seconds off every year. And at that rate, it would take nearly 3500 years to accumulate just one extra day!

Natural Connections

Since early humankind knew there was a definite connection between the Sun and the seasons, they obviously drew the correlation between the Sun and plants. But without the scientific knowledge we enjoy today, this relationship must have seemed rather peculiar at best. Why? Because even though it's a given that ancient farmers expected their seeds to sprout and push through the Earth, and they knew the ground had to be warm to make that happen, it's doubtful that they ever expected more from them than a good crop. However, these young sprouts suddenly seemed to have minds of their own. They turned on their stems to face the Sun—stretching and craning toward Him as if paying homage. It must have seemed as if the plants knew something that the early peoples did not: that the Sun was, indeed, worthy of reverence and adulation. And that behavior pattern may have been the first inkling that the Sun wasn't commonplace at all, but rather a deity in His own right.

It wasn't just the plants, though. Animal behavior changed with the Sun, too. Mammals shed their winter coats as days became warmer, and some of them even changed color. The Sun's new warmth brought a real flurry of activity in the rest of the animal kingdom, too. Cocoons hatched, butterflies burst forth, and fish and turtles became more plentiful. Certain animals suddenly appeared again, even though they hadn't been seen since autumn. Some animals mated, built shelters, and gave birth. Others simply basked in the Sun and soaked up His warmth. It must have seemed as if the Sun Himself was not only responsible for this sudden burst of energy, but also in charge of replenishing the personal power supply.

But that wasn't all. Rainbows appeared after heavy rains, and lit the sky with myriad color. Jewels, when drenched in sunlight, reflected the very same patterns off walls in the form of sunbeams. There were sundogs, too—those rainbowlike arcs occasionally seen at the Sun's corona. And sometimes, the Sun really outdid Himself. He appeared as a big black hole in the sky surrounded by illuminated cross and birdlike patterns.

To the early peoples, this must have truly seemed like magic in the making.

Early Sun Worship

While these things alone were obviously enough to constitute Sun worship in ancient civilization, one can't help but wonder what might have happened if those people had known what we know about the Sun today. Can you imagine, for example, their reaction at knowing that even though the Sun was positioned ninety-three million miles away, He could still light and warm the Earth with ease? Or how they'd have responded to the discovery that He was responsible for every molecule of oxygen they breathed, and every breeze that cooled their bodies? Or what if they knew that He made a large contribution to the health of their bones? Your guess is as good as mine, but one thing's for sure: with the Sun bringing all that magic to the world, they'd probably have worshipped Him much more adamantly than they did. In fact, one has to wonder whether they'd have even bothered to honor anything else at all—or whether the rest of their gods and goddesses would have even existed.

Be that as it may, though, what they *did* know was that the Sun was one of the most powerful forces in their Universe. Some saw Him as the Creator and Life Giver. Others saw Him as the Harbinger of Happiness and Success. And still more saw Him as the absolute Center of the Universe, or the Omnipotent All. Since the Sun was such an important factor in early civilization, though, it's not surprising that variations of His image seemed to turn up everywhere, from temples to tombs, from scrolls to pottery, and from jewelry to other decorative arts.

On the following pages you'll find some of the common Sun symbols utilized by ancient civilization, as well as brief descriptions of their use. It's interesting to note that although some of these symbols are still in use today, their current meanings reach far beyond their original intent. You'll also find that the cross was not initially a Christian symbol at all; in fact, it was important in the religious world long before Christianity was ever conceived. For your convenience, I've divided them into three categories: Solar Symbols, Solar Eclipse Symbols, and Solar Symbol Structures.

Solar Symbols

Circle with Central Dot

This Sun symbol is so ancient that no one seems to be able to accurately pinpoint its timeline. Any time it appears, though—even today—it has something to do with the Sun or His properties. Commonly used today by astrologers to depict the Sun's position in natal charts—and by esoteric astrologers to denote the divine spark of consciousness and co-creationism—it has also been used as the alchemistic symbol for gold, the botanical symbol for plants with a lifespan of one Sun cycle (one year), and as the Cabbalistic symbol for Michael the Archangel, who is associated with both the Sun and Sunday.

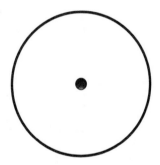

Figure 1: Circle with Central Dot

Quartered Circle

Dating back to about 3000 BC and found in the rock carvings and writings of the Egyptians, Cretians, Etruscans, Greeks, Romans, Chinese,[5] and pre-Columbian Americans, this symbol is commonly known as the Sun Cross. In early times, it not only represented the Sun and ultimate power, but the ruler of the land as well, since he or she was considered to be the Sun's counterpart. (It's interesting to note that the Roman Catholic church uses this symbol in some of its rituals, but calls it the "consecration" or "inaugural" cross. In fact, when the bishop blesses a new church, he anoints the walls in twelve places by drawing this wheel with consecrated water or oil.) The Sun Cross has enjoyed many definitions during its time. It's also known as Odin's Cross, the astronomical symbol for Earth, the astrological symbol for the Part of Fortune, and the solar halo in British meteorological systems.

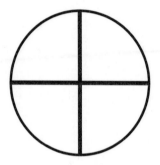

Figure 2: Quartered Circle

Sextant Circle

Another Sun Wheel dating back to the early Bronze Age, this circle image was found in many places during the archaeological excavation of Mohenjo-Daro, which is now a part of modern-day Pakistan. And though all indications point toward its representation of the Sun there, such is not likely elsewhere. The Gauls utilized this symbol as an amulet to gain the protection of their God of Thunder, Taranis. And although Taranis was a solar god in His own right, He certainly was not representative of the Sun in any way. A variation of this image—a circle divided into six portions, with another circle at its center, and the outer rim divided into twelve portions—is the Tibetan symbol for the world wheel.

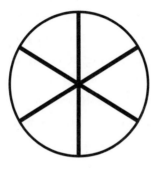

Figure 3: Sextant Circle

Swastika

Since Hitler chose this figure to symbolize the Nazi party during World War II, the swastika[6] has taken a really bad rap over the years. But it wasn't always the symbol of horror we know today. Not only did it originally symbolize the Sun, fire, continuous motion, and the infinite process of creation, but it seemed exclusive to the ancient Sumerians until around 1000 BC. Then it began to crop up in China, Greece, Rome, Egypt, India, and Scandinavia as well. The ancient Minoans used it to symbolize the labyrinth. It's been associated with Artemis, Athena, Astarte, Woden, Freya, and Valkyrja in Her aspect as the Sun warrioress. Also known as St.

Bridget's Cross, it's linked to the Celtic Goddess Bride, in Her Christianized version. Sacred to the Hindu God Ganesha—the remover of all obstacles—this figure is still used today as a talisman to ward off all misfortune. One other notation about the swastika: When it's drawn with the arms pointing to the left,[7] it symbolizes life or the Sun moving in a clockwise motion; drawn with the arms pointing to the right; however, it represents death, or the Moon when moving in a counterclockwise manner. And it's been said that Hitler purposely chose to arm his party with the death symbol even though those closest to him argued that it was a mistake. If that's true, it makes one wonder if he truly expected to triumph at all.

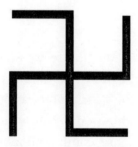

Figure 4: Swastika

Shamash Rosette

Commonly found in the Tigris-Euphrates area around 1000 BC, this rosette was used to represent the Sun, highest divinity, rulership, and the Babylonian Sun God

Shamash. When found rising between the horns in the symbol for Aries, it denotes the Spring Equinox.

Figure 5: Shamash Rosette

Assur Rosette

Found on Assyrian stone sculptures dating back to 850 BC, this rosette is said to have represented Assur, the Creator God, Who in many ways resembled the Baby-lonian God Marduk.

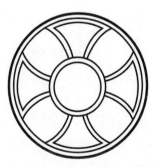

Figure 6: Assur Rosette

Phoenix

The ancient Egyptians often used the phoenix to represent the Sun, Whom they believed died each evening
and was reborn again every morning. It's interesting to
note that this figure was also adopted by the early Christians as a symbol of resurrection and life everlasting.

Figure 7: Phoenix

Solar Eclipse Symbols

Maltese Cross

Found mostly on crowns and royal jewelry throughout the ancient world as early as 2000 BC, astronomers say that this equal-armed cross represents the four flares that extend from the Sun's corona during a solar eclipse.

Figure 8: Maltese Cross

Cross of Marama

Found in Hawaii long before the invasion of John Cook, this Maltese cross is a very good representation of the marriage of the Sun and Moon during the intermediate phase of total eclipse. It's said to be sacred to Marama, an ancient Maori Goddess of Sun and Moon.

Figure 9: Cross of Marama

Winged Disc

Popular in ancient Egypt, this symbol fully resembles the bird pattern formed by the Sun's corona when sunspot activity is at a minimum during the first stages of a solar eclipse. It's also very likely that it was the impetus for wings of Isis, and the hawklike head of the Sun God Ra. (The hawk was sacred to Ra because of its swift travel through the sky.)

Figure 10: Winged Disc

Ankh

Commonly seen as a feminine symbol of everlasting life today, astronomers believe that this image was also originally derived from the birdlike pattern formed in the initial stages of the solar eclipse.

Figure 11: Ankh

Solar Symbol Structures

Obelisk

While we already know that the obelisk was used to mark time, there's more to it than that. In ancient Egypt, for example, it was thought to house the Sun God,[8] and was sacred to Ra. The Canaanites and Phoenicians, however, built the structures to honor Ba'al, a god not only of fertility, but quite possibly a Sun God as well. Whether the latter is true or not is a subject of much debate. (Dissenters say that the confusion is due to the creation of the Hellenistic Sun God Heliogabulus,[9] Who was a combination of Ba'al and the Greek

Sun God Helios.) Be that as it may, though, the obelisk is definitely a structural Sun symbol, and the translation of the word itself is said to be "Ba'al's shaft" or "Ba'al's organ of reproduction."[10] With that in mind, it's interesting to note that the center of the Vatican piazza is graced not just with any obelisk, but one commissioned in the Egyptian city of Heliopolis and sent to Rome by Caligula during his reign as emperor.

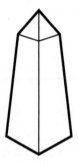

Figure 12: Obelisk

Eight-Spoked Wheel

Because of its eight spokes, this structure bears similarity to the solar rosette used to honor the Babylonian Sun God Shamash. However, it is also akin to the ancient Celtic Sun Wheel, in which the central cross marked the quarter days (the solstices and equinoxes), and the bisecting *X* marked the cross-quarter days (the fire festivals) that made up their solar year. Not only do many pre-Christian ruins reflect this structure, but it is also the structural basis for the Vatican piazza in Rome.

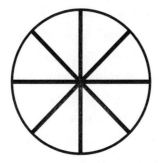

Figure 13: Eight-Spoked Wheel

Solar Gender

Although we think of the Sun as masculine today, such wasn't always the case. In fact, there are probably as many ancient solar goddesses as there are gods. What's more, They enjoyed equal time when it came to worship. Over time, however, these solar goddesses—once important deities in the earliest religious structures—seemed to either fade away or be reinvented, and because of that, Their stories simply got left by the wayside.

But how did these goddesses become connected with the Sun? Who were They? And why were They important?

Most of the early Sun Goddesses were associated with the sky, fire, and beauty, and this formed a definite connection with the Sun. Many were also associated with mirrors, which often took the form of shields. Take the Japanese Sun Goddess Amaterasu, for example, Who was sent to rule the heavens, but was so embarrassed by the errant behavior of Her brother that She hid in a cave instead. The story goes that She was eventually coaxed from the cave by Her own reflection in a mirror, and finally came out to light the world again. Unlike some of the other Sun Goddesses, though, this particular deity still holds a place of importance today, for it's said that she gave birth to the first imperial ruler of Japan—and that all those who followed were directly descended from Her.

Then there was Sunna,[11] the Scandinavian Sun Goddess whose name means "Mistress of the Sun." She rode across the sky in a chariot pulled by Her horses Arvak (early waker) and Alsvid (all strong) while carrying a special shield that kept the Earth safe from Her overpowering rays. To point at the Sun was to pay homage to Sunna. So even if unwittingly, She's still frequently honored today.

And who could forget about the Celtic Sun Goddess Brigid,[12] Whose importance to Her devotees was such that She was canonized by the early Church rather than omitted from its realm? Commonly known as the "Bright One"—and often referred to as "The Bright Fiery Sun"—She was most closely associated with fire and metal-smithing. (In fact, Christian myth has it that in Her role of appointing area bishops, she refused any candidates who could not smith gold.) It's said that shortly after Her birth, a flame burst from Her forehead that reached right into the sky. That story, in and of itself, may have been the initial impetus for the continual tending of Brigid's sacred flame at the shrine at Kildare. When Ireland was Christianized around the fifth century, though, the shrine became a convent. But the sisters of St. Bridget—nuns also known as Brigandines—kept the flame burning until some six hundred years later when the archbishop of Dublin ordered it doused. In 1993, however, the nuns relit the sacred fire, and it now burns continually as a symbol of peace, healing, and well-being.

The Sun Goddess even held a place of importance in Native America, and to the Cherokee people, a nation who never prayed to anyone but the Sun, She was known as Unelanuhi. Legend has it that this goddess lived on the other side of the planet, and the animals had grown weary of living in perpetual darkness. So, after much discussion, they sent the possum to try to catch Her with his curling tail. Unfortunately, though, he came back empty-handed—and all he got for his trouble was a singed appendage. Then the buzzard was sent to bring Her back, but that didn't work either, for Unelanuhi is said to have scorched the feathers right off his head. Finally, the spider decided to give it a shot. She wove a web and snared the Sun, then brought Her back to rest above the Earth. But the story doesn't end there. It goes on to say that Unelanuhi's original position was so close to the Earth that She scorched everything in Her presence. So the elders got together and worked to move Her up in the air until She was seven hands high from the Earth. And it's in that more comfortable position (both for Her and for the rest of us) that She lives to this very day.

Although many other Sun Goddesses come to mind—Saule, Freya, Shakti, Surya, Walu, Sekhmet, Sul, and Aine, just to name a few—Medusa also bears mention here. We know Her as the Greek snake-tressed goddess who was far too horrid to look upon, but this wasn't always the case. It's said, in fact, that She was once quite beautiful and that Her initial role in the mythological system was that of the Anatolian Sun Goddess. And though this is a subject of much debate, it's probably true. Why? Because She's not only associated with the mirror, but gave birth to a creature of the sky (the Pegasus sprang from Her neck as She died). And though Her origins may be argued for centuries to come, this cannot: the battle shield of the Greek Warrior Goddess Athena—Who was frequently thought of as a Sun Goddess Herself—was continually shown adorned with the image of Medusa's head after Her murder.

But if there were just as many Sun Goddesses as Sun Gods, then why don't we think of the Sun as being androgynous instead of masculine?

Truth be told, no one really knows. But if I had to venture a guess, I'd say it probably has something to do with nothing more than good old-fashioned feminine mystique. While it's true that women inherently hold some of the Sun's most basic qualities—things like warmth and nurturance—it's also true that they hold many characteristics basic to the Moon. They're not just radiant beauties, but mysterious creatures. They tend to evoke emotion even when that's not what they intend. And of course, there's the fact that they cycle with the Moon. Tie it all up with the ability to calm everyone in their midst, and you have a veritable Moon creature on your hands.

Men, on the other hand, are a dependable hunting and gathering sort. They defend. They protect. They are physically strong, and loyal champions to those considered worthy of their efforts. What's more, though, they tend to look at things in a simpler, less complex fashion. In their eyes, a situation is usually black or white, with little or no gray in between. And once they make a decision, they lose no time at all in taking action. For all practical purposes, men are a very efficient sort.

Such is the case with the Sun. He's dependable. He gathers what we need—wind, oxygen, light, warmth, and so on—to defend and protect us, and acts as our champion. And unlike the Moon, He doesn't take His sweet time about moving across the sky. Instead, He comes and goes like clockwork and is efficient in His efforts. But even if none of that were true, there's one other thing to be considered: the Sun, being the counterpart of the Moon, is Her exact opposite. And since the Moon is viewed as feminine, it only makes sense for the Sun to be seen as masculine.

While space won't allow for a lengthy or in-depth discussion of all the early Sun Gods, this book simply wouldn't be complete without mentioning a few. So, let's start with Ra. The early Egyptians not only believed that He created light—as well as everything else in the world—but that from His tears sprang the parents of Earth and Sky, Shu and Tefnut. And to this end, they believed that their rulers were also directly descended from Ra. There seems to be some confusion, however, as to whether Ra's devotees truly saw Him as the Sun and all it embodies. Some scholars now say that since Ra was believed to have created everything, it was only His eye that was viewed as the Sun.

Helios was also an important figure since He was, perhaps, the earliest Sun God worshipped by the Greeks. It's said that He drove His golden chariot from east to west in the sky each day, bringing light and warmth to the world. And then, at the end of the day, He took a well-deserved respite by sinking down into the ocean. Of course, this looked like so much fun that His son Phaethon begged to drive the chariot just once. After much debate, Helios agreed. But it wasn't such a wise decision. You see, Phaethon couldn't control the fiery stallions that pulled the chariot; in fact, He was tossed to His death shortly after taking the reins. From that day forward, Helios never let anyone else make the trip across the daytime sky.

The Babylonian Sun God was called Shamash, and though His story is somewhat similar, it doesn't end sadly. As soon as the gates of the east opened each day, Shamash would journey across the sky and work His way toward the western gate. But once He reached His destination, He still couldn't rest. Instead, He hurriedly traveled all night through the underworld. (It was the only route to the eastern gate, and He had to get there in time to bring the next day.) Since His daily journey took Him to such heights across the sky, though, it was believed that He could see *everything*—good or bad—that humankind did. So with that in mind, and with the assumption that Shamash had plenty of time to think about what He'd seen, He was also known as the God of Justice.

The Aztecs had their own Sun God, too. His name was Tonatiuh, and He was very important, indeed. The story goes that there were five Suns created—one for each cosmic age—and that the first four met their demises at the end of their respective eras. The only one left was Tonatiuh, and as such, He was destined to light the world until the end of all time. Like other Sun Gods, though, bringing light and warmth wasn't His only job. He ruled Tollan—an Aztec equivalent of heaven—where only those who died in childbirth or war gained entrance. And because Tonatiuh was also thought to support the entire universe, human sacrifice was often offered to give Him strength.

And then, of course, there was the Celts' God, Lugh, who was also known as "The Shining One." His solar duties, however, only took up a small amount of His

time, for the fact of the matter was that Lugh simply ex-
celled at everything! He fathered Cuculain—a great
Celtic hero—and held dominion over the warrior gods.
He was in charge of the harvest and its bounty, as well.[13]
But His duties didn't stop there. He also handled fertility, prosperity, protection, the arts, and every other sort
of skill imaginable. Why? Because out-and-out excel-
lence was Lugh's forte. Regardless of the challenge,
there was absolutely nothing He couldn't do, and do
well. And maybe that's the real reason He wound up
being so important; in fact, He's the only god that the
Celts worshipped universally.

Many other Sun Gods come to mind here, including
Mithra, Sol Invictus, Apollo, and Ba'al. But regardless
of their names or where they came from, one thing is
certain: Those who worshipped Them felt They were
strong enough and smart enough to handle more than
one job. And so throughout mythology, we find that
every Sun God in existence has not only managed to
juggle His duties without dropping the ball, but has
done a damned fine job of it.

Sunday

What comes to mind when you hear the word "Sunday?" Well, for me, it's usually Christians and sermons
and churches filled to overflow. But that wasn't always
the case. In fact, the actual origins of Sunday worship

are not only rooted in Paganism, but were probably sown and fertilized at the hands of the ancient Romans.

As you'll remember from your high school world history classes, the Romans were credited for naming the days of the week as we know them today. And the first day of the week they named *dies solis,* a Latin phrase meaning "day of the Sun." One of the reasons for this was that they believed the Sun held dominion over all the other planets—or stars, as they called them—and as such, He should be honored by ruling the first day of the week.

Another possible factor for the dictation of Sunday as a sacred holiday may have had to do with Mithraism, the Sun-worshipping cult that was then the official religion of the Roman Empire. Known in Rome as Sol Invictus and in Greece as Helios, this religion honored the Persian Sun God Mithra. And even though Mithra was said to have existed several centuries before the birth of the Christian God Jesus, they shared many parallels. For one thing, Persian mythology holds that Mithra was born of a virgin mother and was known as "the light of the world." For another, His birthday was celebrated on December 25.[14] And after He'd accomplished His mission on Earth—that of teaching brotherly love and compassion—He ate a "last supper" with His friends before "ascending into heaven." Keeping that in mind, it would appear that Mithra actually paved the way for the beginnings of Christiandom.

But I digress. The point is that it only made sense to honor a Sun God on Sunday—it was commonly known as "the Lord's day" and designated as the holiest day of the week—and that's exactly what those in the Roman Empire did.

Interestingly enough, though, the original Christian Sabbath was not held on Sunday at all. It took place, instead, on Saturday, as did the Jewish Sabbath. The reasoning behind this grew from the passage in Genesis in the Old Testament that spoke of God resting on the seventh day. Thus, Saturday was initially the day when no one worked, cooked, did laundry, or anything else, for that matter—except, of course, pray and worship.

If that's the case, though, then how did things get so confused? And what happened to cause the Christians to change their day of worship?

Although nobody really knows for sure, it's likely that it was changed either in order to convert the Pagans or to avoid persecution by blending in with them. And it's quite possible that it all started with Easter, which was always celebrated on Sunday, and began sometime early in the second century. At that point, the Christians took to worshipping at dawn on Sunday and turning toward the east, just as the Mithrasites did. Of course, modern-day Christians now surmise that the intention was to show the Pagans that they weren't worshipping the Sun at all, but honoring their Christ, Who was resurrected at sunrise on Sunday. And since their worship had nothing to do with the Sun, they set Sunday aside as a day of rest rather than one of celebration.

To be perfectly honest, I have serious doubts about the validity of this intention. For one thing, Aurelian officially declared the Sun to be the supreme god of the Roman Empire in AD 274. For another, it's a well-known historical fact that the persecution of the Christians didn't even start to slow down until the spring of 311 with the issue of the Palinode of Galerius;[15] and even then, the edict was frequently ignored. So it only makes sense that the Christians' original idea of embracing Sunday worship had more to do with blending in and avoiding persecution than anything else. And the day of rest thing? Well, while that certainly may have served as justification for the change, I doubt that prudence and good judgment would have allowed for its open proclamation. At least, not at that time.

But when did Sunday observance finally become official? Well, actual dates are a lot more sketchy than you might think. In fact, the first official reference I could find for this had to do with the Council of Elvira held in fourth century Spain—and even then, it was only a reference to temporary excommunication if the Christian missed three Sunday worship services. And the issue wasn't truly addressed until 1917[16] with the Code of Canon Law, which stated that "the faithful" were bound to Sunday worship participation. But that was all it said in regard to Sunday. The question of change and its reason was never fully addressed, and as far as I know, never really has been.

Be that as it may, though, we do know one thing for a fact: The Christian day of worship was changed to come into step with that of the Pagans. And it remains so to this very day.

Other Sun Worship Connections

Christianity became the official religion of the Roman Empire in AD 380, by decree of Emperor Thodosius. But the decree was only a matter of formality, as the new religion had already taken hold and swept through the civilized world. And the Christians had managed this single-handedly—even against all odds—by carefully aligning their religious customs with those of the Sun-worshippers. With most of the Mithrasitic beliefs—including that of eternal life-after-death—already in place, the next step was to assimilate the dates of the major Pagan holidays. The Virgin Mary was introduced, and many of the old gods and goddesses were reborn as saints. The Greek custom of baptism was adopted as well, though it was required at birth or on conversion to cleanse the soul rather than its original purpose: an annual claiming of the regenerative powers of the sea, held every September. And some time later, cathedrals and churches were built on top of ancient Pagan worship sites. This all worked as planned, since the idea was not only to make the Pagans as comfortable as possible, but to prove once and for all that the new religion wasn't all that different from the old one. That being the case, it comes as no surprise that much of the folklore, superstition, and magic that we associate with the Sun also enjoyed church incorporation, and is still alive and well there today.

Take astrology, alchemy, and magic, for example. Thought to have originated in ancient Babylon, these found their way into the church with the introduction of the Magi—members of a caste of Zoroastrian priests who were quite adept at these arts. And since the word "Magi" had come to be defined as "wise" by the first century, they easily gained entrance into the church's history as wise men—and the ancient arts gained entrance as well. That the church eventually denounced these practices is completely irrelevant, for it's accepted by a good many historians and theologians alike that, at least initially, adept knowledge of these arts may have even been a prerequisite to placement in its upper eschalon.

In view of this, it bears mention that Louis XIV actually perpetuated this sort of occultism within the church structure, long after the church denied its use. During his reign, in fact, he provided the means for the construction of a number of alchemistic churches, which reflected his interest in the ancient arts and Pagan philosophy. The French Templars are most famous for the type of church construction Louis preferred: a structure built in the shape of a cross with a circular room attached at the head. And within their walls could be found an absolute treasure trove of solar symbols and devices, from labyrinths to astrological clocks. It's even said that the walls of one of these French churches actually depicted a complete set of the tarot's major arcana, with the original characters exchanged for applicable saints.

But there was more to Louis XIV than that. Interestingly enough, he was known as the Sun King. This wasn't just due to his practice of alchemy and interest in astrology, but to the fact that he brought a prosperity to France that it had never known. And to his people, he seemed to be the very embodiment of the Sun God of old.

Angels, the Queen of Heaven, and the Sun

Although we often think of angels as having taken root in Christianity, such is not the case. Their origins are far older than that—so old, in fact, that each of the archangel's names includes the word "El," which not only means "shining one," but was the name of the ancient Hebrew Sun God predating biblical times. Furthermore, the ancient Egyptians believed that angels were made of fire, and since they were able to take wing and fly across the sky just as the Sun, they were sacred solar creatures. Even more interesting, though, is the fact that the ancient Islamic culture also embraced this school of thought, and together with the Hebrews[17] and

Egyptians, called upon angels to do away with evil and turn bad situations into pleasant ones.

Angels, of course, were never left to their own devices, but were held accountable to a higher power. And the higher power in question was none other than the "Queen of Heaven," known in ancient times by many names, including Ishtar, Inanna, Isis, Asherah, and Shekinah. Today, this goddess is commonly known to Catholics as the Virgin Mary under the guises of "Our Lady of Perpetual Help" and "Queen of the Angels." She is often depicted between the archangels Gabriel and Michael, the latter of whom bears the title of "Defender of the Queen of Heaven" and whose job it is to protect and perpetuate Her worship. What's more, Her clothing is usually either gold trimmed or gold, the color of the Sun.

But what about the fallen angels? Does the Queen of Heaven rule them, too?

Absolutely. In fact, the Virgin Mary was once even known to Hermetics as Mary Lucifer.[18] But the term "fallen angel" as we know it today wasn't even a part of the picture until Christianity took hold. And that was only because angels were thought to bring unique gifts to humankind—some of which were the knowledge of astrology, psychism, herbalism, and magic—and it suddenly became necessary to separate the Church from all things occult. (As an aside, it was also believed that angels had the ability to couple with the human female—and it just wouldn't do for the church to condone that, either!) So, Lucifer—Who was known as "The Bringer of Light" and was regularly called upon for aid in matters of transformation—"fell from grace," and took a legion of other angels with him. By demonizing Lucifer's group—and giving the group sole responsibility for bringing the ancient arts to humankind—this struck a necessary balance. For one thing, it left the other angels blameless and able to distribute their less harmful gifts to humankind. (Since angels had been long thought of as fortunate creatures, it wouldn't have been a good idea to stamp them out completely.) But more importantly, it was the avenue by which the gods of the past began to become the demons of the new religion. And that in itself was a giant step toward the eradication of Pagandom.

If we look at the Hermetic school of thought, though, we find that the term "fallen angel" enjoys a completely different sort of definition. There, we find that fallen angels are those who *choose* to come to Earth and help humankind of their own volition. I, for one, see more truth in this definition than in the other. We've all heard of cases where angels have purportedly aided those in crisis. And I see no reason why this sort of aid—the same sort that was attributed to *all* angels for literally hundreds of thousands of years—should suddenly be relegated to only a few.

Still, many practitioners shy away from evoking angelic assistance in their workings. And while this is probably due to the more modern connection to Christianity, this is very sad, indeed. Why? Because angels will aid anyone—Pagan, Christian, or otherwise—who asks for their help. And refusing to call on these ancient creatures of the Sun could make all the difference between an absolutely spectacular working or one that's nothing more than adequate.

Sun Worship Today

No book of this type would be complete without at least touching on the religious festivals that we associate with Sun worship today. And while it's true that all eight Sabbats are, indeed, fire festivals—and thus, somewhat related to the Sun—there are many excellent books already available that provide a detailed look at these connections. For this reason, I'd like to look at only two festivals.

At this point, I can almost hear the wheels turning in your head and see you whip your neck around to look at me in amazement. I can almost hear what you're thinking, too. Coupled with a wagging finger, it would go something like, "TWO? Only TWO? But that's not right. There are FOUR!"

And right you are—well, sort of. While Spring and Fall Equinox are, indeed, associated with the Sun, that is not where their main strengths lie. The equinoxes bring the balance of light and dark, and as such, their strengths lie in one just as much as the other.

The solstices, on the other hand, are an entirely different story. Each is intrinsically wrapped up in the Sun; so much so, in fact, that without Him, there would be no need for the solstices at all. And that would be a real shame. Aside from the fact that our Yule and Midsummer celebrations would cease to exist, there would be no start date for Winter or Summer. The seasons would get all fouled up and . . . well . . . suffice it to say that the Sun is truly the shining star of both festivals, and we're very glad that He continues to make an appearance.

Yule or Winter Solstice

Based on ancient Winter festivals of many origins and generally occurring on either December 20 or 21, the Winter Solstice marks the shortest day of the year. And for many of us, its Yule celebration also marks the birth of the newborn Sun.

The manner in which people celebrate this festival varies from tradition to tradition and culture to culture. One of the most common themes, however, comes from the Celts and involves a raging battle between the Kings of Holly and Oak. The old Holly King (a symbol of the aging darkness of the old year) is eventually defeated by the young Oak King. And with His victory, the world comes alive once more with new light and warmth.

Other solstice traditions are a bit more generic, and seem to concentrate more on the birth of the Sun Itself. I'm aware, for example, of several groups that gather outdoors on solstice morning just before sunrise. And just as day begins to break, the members assume the roles of Mother Earth's birthing coaches. They scream and yell—urging the Mother on and the baby forward—until at last, the Sun is pushed into the sky and rests securely where He can accumulate strength during the coming months.

Regardless of the precise way this festival is celebrated, though, one thing is sure: the central theme is one of light and warmth. And the Sun—Who is birthed anew on this day each year—is more than happy to oblige.

Midsummer or Summer Solstice

Also known as Litha, Summer Solstice heralds the first day of Summer, is the longest day of the calendar year, and generally occurs on June 21 or 22. According to many Pagan traditions, this day marks the time when the God becomes an adult, reaches His prime, and takes His rightful place as Father Sun (or the Holly King). The Goddess, in turn, becomes Mother Earth, and dancing together, They green the world with the rich, lush, abundant bounty that will feed Their children at the Fall harvest.

Another common thread is the Battle of the Lords Light and Dark. In this skirmish, the Dark Lord tries to steal the pregnant Goddess, but is waylaid by the Light Lord. The fight ensues—light against dark, dark against light—until the Dark Lord's sword finally hits its mark, slashing the chest of His Brother, the Light. While the Light Lord is weakened, He is still at his peak, so He manages to overpower His Brother, the Dark. A perfect hero, He saves the day for the Goddess and Her unborn Child. All do not live happily ever after, though. Since the Light Lord never quite recovers from the wound of the Dark, His light grows weaker with each passing day until the rematch scheduled for Yule.

Because of the underlying themes of the related stories, most people see Midsummer as a celebration of service, of sharing, and of making restitution. And for this reason, you'll often find these festivities aligned with a charity fundraiser, a group effort to feed the hungry, or a clothing/toy drive for needy children. But that's not all. You see, it's said that the fey are at their prime during the solstice, too, so you're also likely to see festival-goers tossing a dime here or there to keep the fairies at bay.

Sun Superstitions

Anything with the power to infiltrate all societies from the dawn of civilization and never manage to wane once in strength to the present is bound to be veiled with all sorts of related beliefs. Such is the case with the Sun. And because most of these beliefs have absolutely no basis in fact—some are just absurd and others were introduced by the church to stamp out Sun worship—I've listed them here for your amusement.

Please note, however, that a few of these are not ridiculous at all and do have some basis in either common sense or fact. Some of the weather predictors do ring true, for example, and I can certainly see the spiritual value of including a Sun symbol for luck during a baptismal ceremony.

So, laugh where you will and gather what you may. I leave what may be of future worth entirely up to you.

Agriculture

- If the Sun shines through the apple trees on Christmas or Easter day, the fruit yield for the year will be great. (It's also said to bring exemplary luck to those who own the trees.)

Babies

- Babies born in the early morning hours will live a longer life than those born later in the day.

- A baby born at sunrise is gifted with a high intellect and life-long success.

- A baby born at sunset will grow up to be lazy and have absolutely no ambition.

- In India rice is scattered on the ground in the form of the Swastika at the baptism of a baby boy; this practice is said to bring him a lucky life.

Bad Luck

- Apparently, it's very unlucky to point at the Sun—but no one seems to know what will happen if you do.

- If you don't want to die, never stand where the Sun can shine directly on you at a funeral. If you do, it's said that death will claim you soon, as well.

- To move or dance in a circle against the motion of the Sun (counterclockwise) isn't just unlucky; it's said to invite the powers of darkness into one's life.

- Never turn a mattress on a Sunday; it's said to bring nightmares—and other bad things—to those who sleep on it.

Cooking

- If jellies, jams, sauces, gravies, and candy are not stirred Sunwise (clockwise), they will be completely inedible.

Marriage

- According to Hungarian legend, single women should never sweep dust in the direction of the Sun. If they do, they'll never be brides.

- If the Sun shines on a bride on her wedding day, the marriage will be a happy one.

Truth

- Cornish superstition has it that the Sun has absolutely no patience with liars; in fact, it's said that

He'll neither warm them nor cast light upon them with His rays.

Weather

- If the Sun brings unseasonable heat on Christmas day, fires will be a problem for the next twelve months.

- In the marshy area of Lincolnshire, a bucket of water was put out at sunrise on Easter Sunday to divine the weather of the season. If the first rays shined directly on the water and brought a steady reflection, it heralded a mild and favorable season. But even the slightest waver in the reflection foretold a cold, wet, and nasty season.

Endnotes

1. This is very important stuff, because proper calcium absorption prevents osteoporosis.

2. Even though we often refer to the Sun as a planet, He is actually a star.

3. A stone structure thought to be the oldest time-keeper in existence is approximately six thousand years old and still stands in Nabta, Egypt. The Great Cheops Pyramid—built several centuries later—is also thought to measure time.

4. In AD 1200, an Arab mathematician named Abu al-Hasan figured this out, and introduced equal hours to the timeline.

5. While this symbol definitely represented power in Ancient China, historical experts now believe that it was associated more with energy, respect, and thunder than with the Sun.

6. Swastika is derived from the Sanskrit words *su,* meaning "good," and *asti,* meaning "to be."

7. Even though the arms point to the left, this figure is known as the "right-handed" version. The reason is that the arms must trail behind as rudders to provide the trajectory necessary for clockwise motion.

8. James Hall, *Illustrated Dictionary of Symbols in Eastern and Western Art* (Boulder, CO: Westview Press, 1996), 75.

9. This Sun God was possibly created through the deification of the Roman Emperor by the same name who ruled from AD 218–222.

10. Cathy Burns, *Masonic and Occult Symbols* (Mt. Carmel, PA: Sharing Publishers, 1998), 341.

11. Patricia Monaghan, *The New Book of Goddesses and Heroines* (St. Paul, MN: Llewellyn Publications, 1989), 287.

12. Upon canonization, the Church changed Her name to Bridget.

13. Lughnasad is named for Lugh.

14. In AD 354, this date was claimed for the birth of the Christ-child by the Roman bishop, Liberius, and used as a tool to convert the masses to Christianity.

15. Issued by Emperor Galerius, this edict forbade further persecution of Christians and gave them free rein to worship as they saw fit.

16. Greg Dues, *Catholic Customs & Traditions: A Popular Guide* (Mystic, CT: Twenty-Third Publications, 1994), 27.

17. The Seals of Solomon were designed specifically to "collect" the entities who wreaked havoc upon the world, and render their evil-doing harmless.

18. Mary Magdalene was also known by this title in France.

2

Bringing Good Things to Light

When it comes to planning magical efforts, our first thoughts usually involve the Moon. We grab the ephemeris and check Her phases. We look at Her astrological sign and determine whether She's void of course. And once we finally find a day when everything in the lunar realm meets with our exact set of specifications, we gather our tools and get busy. Why? Because everyone knows that the only sure-fire way to magical success is to work in harmony with the Moon. Right?

Well, not exactly. While working in harmony with the Moon can definitely level the odds of magical success—and most practitioners *do* prefer to go that route—this line of thinking can also cause some real problems when it comes to using the magical arts in our busy world. How? Because we have to wait for the perfect Moon conditions. We have to put things on hold until She decides to cooperate. And this can be a very time-consuming process, indeed.

Fact is, most of us don't have that sort of time—especially when it comes to performing magical efforts. When we need cash, we need it now. When we need protection, it can't wait until next week. And when we finally get around to inviting that perfect love into our lives, we really don't want to put it off for several months. Unfortunately, though, this is the sort of waiting game we all have to play if we expect the Moon to level our odds. And this is one of the reasons that many practitioners just muddle through life on their own. They simply don't have time to wait around for the right magical conditions to avail themselves, so they discount magic entirely, and just accept whatever life throws their way.

This sort of thinking is not only a shame—but a shame of the worst sort. Why? Because the correct magical conditions are actually in place every single day. We just don't see them because we're so concerned about the Moon's activities that we've forgotten how to think outside the box.

The Mystical Magical Sun

I first started working with the Sun when one of my students questioned the relevance of His force in magical endeavors. He reasoned that as the counterpart of the Moon, the Sun was not only magically valid as the culmination of all male energies, but brought properties to spell work that we seldom used. To say that his statement gave me pause for thought would be putting it lightly. I was absolutely speechless. Why? Because even after all my years in the Craft, I'd never really thought about why our tradition—one that expressly taught the duality of Godhead and perfect balance—placed such little significance on the Sun and His properties. But after further discussion, I agreed to research the subject and get back to him.

And what did I find? Almost nothing. Oh, I found plenty about using the energies of the Moon. And there was a ton of stuff related to Element work. But when it came to the Sun, there was nothing even remotely pertinent. Unless, of course, you considered adding a Sun symbol to the work at hand. And even then its use was only to bring success to the effort. The Sun was definitely getting the short end of the magical stick on this one, and it just didn't make any sense.

So, armed with nothing but the mission at hand, my stubborn streak, and some old spell books (the Internet hadn't been invented yet), I decided to explore His energies myself. I just knew that a force as powerful as the Sun—a force that brought so much to our daily lives—deserved some real validation in the magical realm. And I was determined to find it.

Sunrise and Sunset seemed like good places to start, so I worked with them much as I normally did with the waxing and waning phases of the Moon. And in doing so, I discovered that the Sun and Moon had lots of energies in common, but were miles apart in other areas.

The most apparent, of course, had to do with the fact that the Sun was warm and the Moon was cool. The illumination factors were different as well, with the Sun's light being much stronger. And then there was the way the energies felt. While lunar energies often seemed complex and somewhat convoluted, solar energies were much simpler in nature. In fact, they were direct and to the point. They provided more of a "what you see is what you get" type of atmosphere, and as such, left the practitioner feeling more sure of the end result.

But the cosmic light bulb really came on when I realized something that should have been clear all along. Simply put, it's this: The Sun moves through different phases all day long, where the Moon takes much longer to complete Her path. And using this constant flow of Sun energy avails the practitioner of nearly any magical influence necessary, regardless of the effort. There's no muss. No fuss. No waiting on pins and needles. All we have to do is be ready to go when the proper Sun phase arrives. It's as simple as that.

Finding Your Place in the Sun

If you've never worked with Sun phases—or don't have much experience with them—it's a good idea to attune yourself to their energies before using them magically. Why? Because there's nothing worse than getting the surprise of your life right in the middle of a magical effort. And getting in touch with the specific phases will go a long way toward preventing that. You'll know what each energy feels like and what to expect. More importantly, though, attunement provides a bond with the god aspects of the Sun and helps you to develop a firm relationship with them. And a good rapport with the Sun God is important stuff—especially when you're asking for His help! (For your convenience, ideas for getting to know each phase follow.)

The Infant/Young Child Sun

The Infant or Young Child Sun is enthusiastic, courageous, and self-confident. He embraces the world with wild abandon. It is, after all, a wonderful place filled with awesome treasures and uncharted territories just begging to be discovered. And since society hasn't managed to indoctrinate Him with its expectations yet, He fears absolutely nothing—even the things that He probably should. For all practical purposes, this Sun is the Inner Child.

To attune yourself to the Infant or Young Child, think back to your childhood. Conjure up memories of a time that was simpler and easier—a time when all your hurts could be healed with a Band-Aid, a kiss, and a Tootsie Roll Pop. Then think about the things that you really enjoyed doing. Better yet, make a list. Some ideas might include:

• Skipping stones, wading in the creek, or skinny-dipping.

- Playing on swings, seesaws, or riding the merry-go-round.

- Skipping rope, playing jacks, or shooting marbles.

- Running in the wind, just for the fun of it.

- Chewing bubblegum and blowing bubbles—even though your mother said it was rude.

- Drawing, coloring, cutting and pasting, or working on an arts and crafts project that incorporates all of these.

Once you've written everything down, pick an item each day and take a few minutes to fully embrace it. You'll be in step with this Sun in no time flat.

The Adolescent Brother/Lover Sun

The Adolescent Brother or Lover Sun is a young, strapping, gorgeous specimen of masculinity. There's no risk too great, no challenge too difficult. In fact, there's absolutely nothing He can't do—or so His hormones tell Him. That's because this Sun is at the height of His sexual peak. For this reason, the Adolescent Brother or Lover Sun speaks to us of both expansion and romance.

To align yourself with this Sun, think back to the time when you were seventeen or eighteen. Go back to the days when you were invincible, when you thought you were ten feet tall and bulletproof. Remember how nothing was impossible, how everything was fun, and how goals were nothing more than victories you hadn't yet achieved. And, of course, don't forget about love and romance and sex, which were right up there on the top of the list, as well.

After your trek down memory lane, look at the list of activities below and add a few of your own.

- Give a hug, tell a joke, or make someone smile.

- Step up to the plate in someone else's defense—or maybe even your own.

- Invite some friends to go skating, go out for a soda or sundae, or just grab a burger.

- Ask someone out on a date; if you're married or committed, ask your partner.

- Kiss at the movies, and don't worry if anyone's watching.

- Take your date parking and neck in the car. Then go home and make wild passionate love—maybe even in the kitchen!

Once you've finished adding to the list, pick one thing to do each day, and you'll be dancing with the Adolescent Brother or Lover Sun before you know it.

The Father Sun

The Father Sun is just that: the Eternal Father. He loves His children regardless of whether they're right or wrong or indifferent. He's also a good provider, and makes sure that His children have what they want as well as what they need. But what about discipline? Well, He handles that, too. But His sort of discipline isn't what you might think; it comes through teaching us and guiding us in the direction necessary to become responsible adults. This Sun also understands that laughter is usually the best medicine, so a relationship with Him is always filled with smiles and winks and plenty of chuckles.

To get in touch with the Father Sun, think back to the time you first began to rear your family. If you don't have children, not to worry. Simply visualize what it would be like to have them. Think about the responsibilities involved, the love shared, and the daily joys that your children could bring. Also, think about your own parents, how they treated you, and what you would do differently when placed in the role of responsible parenthood.

Once you've finished collecting your thoughts, look at the list of activities below and add a few of your own.

- If you have children, give your partner the day (or evening) off and spend some quality time alone with them. Make it a fun time. Play games, laugh, chat, and eat together.

- If you don't have children, borrow your nieces, nephews, or the neighborhood kids for the previous exercise.

- Give some time to organizations that mentor children. (Spiral Scouts and Big Brothers Big Sisters of America come to mind here, but there may be other good organizations in your area.)

- Visit a children's hospital and spend a little time with the patients there. If you have a family, bring them along and make it a fun-filled outing.

- If you excel in sports, offer to coach a children's team of some type.

- Offer to teach a children's class at the local community center. Regardless of the talents you may have, both the children and the center will appreciate your time.

Once you've made personal additions to the list, pick an item and see it through. When the task is completed, pick another. Father Sun will be smiling on you in no time at all.

The Sage/Warrior Sun

The Sage or Warrior Sun is an interesting character, for He holds the best of both worlds: that of wisdom and strength. For this reason, He's neither quick to anger, nor an advocate of brute force. Instead, He calculates and strategizes—rolling things over and over in His mind—until He can determine whether a battle is truly necessary. Sometimes it is, and sometimes it isn't. Regardless of what He decides, though, He always finds a solution that benefits all. And often, He finds that it comes in the form of good advice, clear communications, and a calming of fears. This Sun also knows that time is a precious commodity, and that its waste is equivalent to a loss of strength and power.

To step into place with the Sage or Warrior Sun, think back to some of the most difficult times in your life. Play them back objectively like an old movie and pay careful attention to how you handled them. Think about how a different solution might have changed your life or the lives of those involved, and determine whether you'd handle things differently should the situation arise again.

Once you've finished the inner journey, look at the list of activities below and add a few of your own.

- Make a list of decisions that you need to make in the next week, and write down how you plan to handle each. Then examine your solutions carefully to see whether they'll benefit everyone involved.

- Draw up an emergency plan to be used in the event of a natural disaster such as an earthquake, fire, tornado, flood, or hurricane. Don't forget emergency provisions for any pets, or other provisions such as canned food, flashlights and batteries, bottled water, and cash.

- Take up a cause that you can fully embrace. Some ideas might include animal conservation, something with an ecological or environmental slant, or maybe even a neighborhood recycling project.

- Volunteer a few hours a week at a homeless shelter, a women's shelter, an animal shelter, or a center for the terminally ill. See what you can do to calm fears and make the lives of the residents better.

- Offer your ear to friends and family. Be available when they need a shoulder, a hug, or sound advice. In helping others, we often hone our own decision-making skills, and thus we help ourselves.

Once you've made some personal additions to the list, pick an item and see it through. When the task is completed, pick another.

The Grandfather/Sacrificial Sun

The Grandfather or Sacrificial Sun is past His prime. But that doesn't mean that He's not important. Nothing could be further from the truth. Fact is, He's seen it all, done it all, and knows what's worth trying again. Because of that, He possesses a joy and wisdom that surpasses that of the other Sun phases. He knows when it's time to hold tight, and when it's time to let go. But most of all, He understands that the latter is necessary to make room for the new, and as such, He's willing to sacrifice Himself for the good of all as He slowly sinks below the horizon.

This is perhaps the most difficult Sun to get a handle on because doing so forces us to take a long, hard look at our own mortality. And that's just not high on our priority lists of fun things to do. However, attuning yourself to the Grandfather or Sacrificial Sun isn't just about endings. It's also about memories made, risks taken, and goals achieved. So, start by taking a look at all the wonders that have filled your life. Think about connections made—even those fleeting ones—and the roles they played in your transformation. Look at your accomplishments, too, and give yourself a well-deserved pat on the back. And while you're at it, be sure to think about what you've done for others over the years, and how even your smallest kindnesses impacted their lives and brought about the changes necessary for their personal metamorphoses. Know that you have a lot to be proud of.

Once you've finished reminiscing, look at the list of activities below and add a few of your own.

- Simplify your life by gathering old and useless possessions. Toss out anything that's broken or worn-out. Then either have a yard sale with the rest, or box up the leftovers and give them to a charity for distribution to the needy.

- Draw up your will. Even if you don't think you're old enough to do that just yet, give some thought to who you'd trust to handle your affairs, and who you'd want to have your prize possessions when you're gone. (You may also want to think about medical instructions if you wind up being incapacitated.) Write it all down and put the will in a safe place for future reference. Be sure to alert family members to its whereabouts.

- Share stories of your life with friends and family members, and don't forget to include those of ancestors with whom you're familiar. Better yet, write them all down and make a booklet of sorts to distribute to your loved ones.

- Make a list of all the things that weigh heavily on your mind. Release the ones that simply don't matter—we all have some of those—by scratching them out. Then take steps to handle the others one at a time. Cross off each task as it's completed, and know that you handled it correctly.

- Banish worry and guilt from your life. Neither has ever been known to bring resolution; in fact, both are an absolute waste of time. Resolve, instead, to live your life joyfully. Handle difficult situations as they come, but don't dwell on them. Most importantly, though, take time every day to smile and laugh. Life will not only become more fun, but you'll live a lot longer as well!

Once you've made some personal additions to the list, pick an item and see it through. When the task is completed, pick another.

Since the phases of the Sun have distinctly different magical properties, a brief description of each follows below for your convenience. But please don't stop there. I urge you to explore these wonderful energies for yourself. Work with them. Experiment with them. Invite them on a personal magical journey. While your findings will certainly include the properties outlined below, others may surface as well. And those that do may be so magnificent and so potent that you'll never see magic in the same way again!

Dawn: Infant/Young Child Sun

Because this phase belongs to the Child, it's a very important one, indeed. In fact, it lends itself to virtually anything connected to fresh starts, beginnings, or change. That being the case, try it for efforts involving new jobs, new loves or relationships, new directions in life, or new perspectives. Rejuvenation efforts such as a renewal of hope and trust, a reclamation of personal joy, or a recovery of good health or physical energy are also good bets now, too. In fact, even a broken heart can benefit from this energy, for nothing else has the mending or refreshing abilities of the Rising Sun. Need to consecrate a new tool, ritual space, or some candles? Now's the time to do it. (The only exception is the cup, which is inherently attuned to Water and the Moon.)

Because the Sun rises in the east, I like to face that direction when using this phase. I've also discovered that working outdoors where you can actually see the Sun rise seems to boost magical power. If that's not possible, though, don't fret. Just work from a window facing east—or one that allows you to see the Sun crop up over the horizon—and call it good.

For an additional boost of power, invoke the energies of the Infant/Young Child Sun before beginning your work by saying something like:

O Youngest Babe, so newly born
Help me on this bright new morn

Aid this effort with Your power
And strengthen it with every hour

Morning: Adolescent Brother/Lover Sun

The energy of the Sun expands during the morning hours, making it very strong and active. This means that any project that requires building, growth, or expansion works exceedingly well during this phase. It provides an excellent time to build upon the positive aspects in your life, to resolve situations where courage is necessary, and to bring warmth and harmony to home, family, and relationships. Since anything involving increase works well now, too—and because the metal of the Sun is gold—this energy simply can't be beat for working toward uninhibited cash flow. Don't discount it for gardening matters either, for plant magic performed in the morning hours produces absolutely magnificent results. But that's not all. It also offers the perfect conditions for working with matters of the heart, so if you're having issues with romance or sex, or you just need to bring that freshly-in-love feeling back into a relationship, now's the time to handle the problem.

For an additional boost of power, invoke the energies of the Adolescent Brother or Lover Sun before beginning your work by saying something like:

O Vital Sun of growing strength
Come to me and stay at length

Bring my work intensity
And add to it Your potency

Noon: Father Sun

The energies of the Sun claim full power as He peaks the sky at high noon. And as such, this is the time to turbocharge most any magical effort that comes to mind. Along with the more complicated matters normally reserved for Full Moon—matters of the heart, and those dealing with finances, justice, and protection come to mind here—I've also found this energy to be unsurpassed when it comes to charging crystals and metal ritual tools such as the athame, boline, and censor. It also provides an excellent time for health magic, and for bringing that extra burst of vigor, strength, and personal energy necessary to get through the day's to-do list. Don't discount it, either, for matters involving study and knowledge retention, or for those that require extreme illumination and magnification.

For an additional boost of power, invoke the energies of the Father Sun before beginning your work by saying something like:

Father Sun of strength and might
Aid this work in taking flight
To the target, be its guide
And add your power to its ride

Afternoon: Sage/Warrior Sun

As the Sun journeys downward from its peak, its energies become more receptive, less brash, and much more discerning. This is a good phase to handle projects that need clarity and resolution, but require a strategic approach with a soft touch. Professionalism, business matters, communications, and all interactions with other people fall into this category. Rituals concerning the exploration of new ideas, adventures, and travel are most successfully performed during this phase, as are those that involve the acquisition of personal wisdom or tenacity, and the skills to cut through deceit. A very versatile Sun, the Sage or Warrior even provides a good time to balance the checkbook.

It's important to note that even though this Sun is in His waning stages, the energy He exudes is nothing like that of the Waning Moon. (It's much more tenacious than that of its lunar counterpart, and still enjoys a warm sort of strength that She can't boast.) For this reason, I don't suggest using it for the breakage of bad habits or any sort of banishment.

For an additional boost of power, invoke the energies of the Sage or Warrior Sun before beginning your work by saying something like:

Wise Warrior Sun of Amber Light
Wrap me in Your rays so bright
And wrap my work within them, too
So it hits its mark, both straight and true

Sunset: Grandfather/Sacrificial Sun

This Sun is much akin to the waning stage of the Moon in that its predominant energies vibrate toward conditions that need to be diminished or alleviated entirely. This makes it a good time to set life simplification plans in motion or to tie up loose ends. Need to cleanse something? Whether it's a tool or stone, a ritual space or yourself, now is the time to do it. There's more. The Grandfather or Sacrificial Sun also provides the perfect atmosphere for work that involves dieting, getting rid of bad habits, and completely eradicating personal aggravations like stress, confusion, and poor health. Efforts designed to uncover deceptions of any type work well now, too, as do those related to divinatory skills and psychism. In fact, nearly anything that can be done during the Waning Moon enjoys great success during this phase.

When working in harmony with the Grandfather or Sacrificial Sun, I've found that facing west while working outdoors seems to raise success rates. If that's not a viable option, though, try to work from a window where you can see Him sink below the horizon—and know that He takes your problems with Him as He descends.

For an additional boost of power, invoke the energies of the Grandfather or Sacrificial Sun before beginning your work by saying something like:

> *O Setting Sun of passing day*
> *Aid me in your gentle way*

Take this effort, Ancient One
With Your strength as You pass on

Occasional Sun Magic

While most Sun phases avail themselves to us each and every day, there are a few that come much less frequently. And because of this, we await them with great anticipation. Some of them are predictable, so they are a little easier to prepare for magically. Others are not; in fact, we have no idea when they might appear, so using them in magical efforts can be a little trickier. Our only option is to be ready to go when they grace us with their presence. Even worse, there are those—the sundog comes to mind here—that only last mere seconds, and are already gone before you can even say, "So mote it be." They don't allow the time necessary for magical work at all, and that can be more than just a bit aggravating.

Since there's no point in teasing you with phases too fleeting to use in your efforts, I've chosen to exclude them entirely. Instead, we'll only work here with those that last long enough to be of use. You shouldn't, after all, have to be a marathon runner to use them magically, and there's certainly no point in raising your blood pressure if you miss them. Besides, a relaxed practitioner is an effective practitioner. And that's exactly what you want to be.

Rainbows

Since the beginning of time, rainbows have enjoyed an excellent reputation in both folklore and religious mythology. According to Christian myth, a rainbow is a reminder that the world shall never again be destroyed by flooding. To the Celts, it speaks of joy, happiness, and prosperity. (Who, after all, wouldn't be absolutely ecstatic after finding a pot of gold at its end?) The ancient Greeks, though, held an entirely different view. They believed that it was a symbol of their goddess Iris, Who held dominion over the bridge between life and death, and reminded all that the cessation of physical life was a joyful experience. Regardless of myth or legend, though, rainbows are always seen as a good omen.

But what causes a rainbow? And what role does the Sun play in its formation?

While tons of scientific data is readily available on the formation of rainbows, there's no point in going into all of that here. A simpler explanation is in order, and that has to do with the combination of light and water. Because sunlight is a combination of all the colors that the eye can register, its light is considered white. And when it shines through a raindrop, it acts much like a prism, causing a separation of the seven basic colors—red, orange, yellow, green, blue, indigo, and violet—visible to the eye.

This phenomenon differs somewhat from that of the prism, though. Instead of seeing the round sunbeam that comes from the prism, we see an arc. And that has to do with the shape of the raindrop and the unique way in which it refracts the light. Because raindrops are spherical in shape, the light has to bend in order to refract, and once this happens, the raindrop forms a series of colored arcs. We get an arched band of color separations instead of a round one, and a rainbow is reflected in the sky. It's as simple as that.

How often do rainbows occur, though? Is there any way to predict one?

Unfortunately, rainbows just seem to have a mind of their own. Sometimes they appear, and sometimes they don't. It's one of those infrequent phases that always comes as a total surprise. And thus, it's one that we have to be ready for magically.

While we usually view the presence of a rainbow as one of life's little treasures, something quite phenomenal happens on occasion. Rainbows will form in double and triple patterns. It's simply a matter of the sunlight being reflected more than once within the same raindrop, or sometimes, within several. But since this is a very infrequent occurrence, indeed, I find it of major magical importance to the practitioner. Why? Because any magic performed during these periods simply can't help but be doubled or tripled in power.

The rainbow can be used for any number of things in the magical arena, but since the seven basic colors are at the forefront—the same seven that represent the chakras—rainbow periods provide an excellent time for all sorts of chakra work and healing, including those efforts that require the use of reiki and sekhem. Anything requiring balance is a good bet, too, and because the Sun is always at your back when viewing a rainbow, it also provides the perfect atmosphere for meditations designed to dispell stress, depression, and anxiety. Working with the terminally ill in some form? Call on Iris to provide an exceptional journey across the bridge. And don't discount the value of a quick money spell during this phase, either. The Celts very well may have been on to something!

Solar Eclipses

Solar eclipses only occur at the New Moon during Her journey between the Earth and the Sun. And while it's perfectly logical to think that we'd have an eclipse at least once per month, it just doesn't happen that way. Why? Because the Moon's orbit around the Earth is more slanted than the Earth's orbit around the Sun. And for this reason, the Moon's shadow usually misses the Earth's surface entirely. About twice a year, though, things line up just right and we have a solar eclipse: a brief period when at least a part of the Moon's shadow passes over the Sun.

There are two kinds of solar eclipses, and the determining factor has to do with which shadow of the Moon is involved. A *partial solar eclipse* comes about when the Moon offers Her penumbra, or Her light, outer shadow.

While I find partial eclipses a little unbalancing and prefer not to perform magical efforts then, such may not
be the case for you. In fact, you may want to experiment
with the energies a bit. And if you choose to go that
route, efforts that involve the personal journey or require tying up loose ends might work well. Experiencing
a partial eclipse up close and personal might be a good
idea, though, before using its energies in the magical
realm. That way, you'll know exactly how the energies
affect you, and won't have any unpleasant surprises
while you're knee-deep in ritual.

A *total eclipse of the Sun*, however, occurs when the
umbra—or the darker, inner shadow of the Moon—
comes into play. The shadow of the Moon completely
covers the surface of the Sun, blocking out most of His
light, and causing a temporary darkness that slightly resembles the twilight period of early evening. Only the
corona of the Sun—or His halo—is visible on the outside of the Moon's shadow, and often forms interesting
patterns of light against the darkened sky. Scholars say
that it's these patterns that were the origin of many ancient Sun symbols, including the ankh, the winged disk,
and the phoenix.

Magically speaking, the total eclipse symbolizes a
consummation of the marriage between the Sun and
the Moon. This means that its energies are not only extremely balanced, but unsurpassed in strength and effectiveness. More to the point, they provide the perfect
atmosphere for efforts involving relationships, matters

of the heart, justice, and general, personal, or financial balance.

There's good news and bad news about the total eclipse, though. And just for grins, I'll give you the bad news first: not everybody can see the total eclipse when it occurs. That's because you must be within the Moon's path of totality—usually a distance of about a thousand miles long by a hundred miles wide—in order to view it. Which portion of the world enjoys this phenomenon depends solely upon the position of the Moon when She casts Her shadow.

The good news? Solar eclipses are not only entirely predictable, but the portions of the world capable of viewing them are always listed with their time and date. And this means that you'll have plenty of time to prepare for them magically whenever they decide to grace you with their presence.

Sun Storms

We seldom think of weather conditions as causing problems anywhere other than here on Earth. In fact, we seldom even consider that there is any sort of weather anywhere else. But that's just not so. Outer space has its own sort of weather, too, and Sun storms can definitely wreak havoc with it.

Sun storms are geomagnetic and caused by a series of eruptions and explosions on the Sun's surface. These explosions emit lots of tiny particles that fly into space at speeds in excess of a thousand miles per hour, and set course for Earth's atmosphere. And since they're both radioactive and magnetized, they wreak havoc here, too, when they arrive.

So, what kinds of problems do they cause? Because they're highly magnetized, they can screw up compass readings and interfere with global positioning systems. (The latter, of course, is a real problem since most air traffic controllers use the GPS to track airplanes on the radar.) They also have the ability to knock out power systems and cause blackouts, push satellites out of orbit, and interrupt radio transmissions. And if that weren't enough, this solar fallout also brings a hefty dose of radiation with its arrival; in fact, flying on a day when Sun storms are in progress often brings travelers ten times the radiation of a normal chest x-ray.

Be that as it may, though, the energies of these aggravating little storms can be very effective when harnessed for magical use. Because of the magnetized particles involved, they're absolutely unsurpassed in power when it comes to attraction magic. In fact, nearly any magic worked during these periods comes to fruition quickly, provided that the desired result is visualized as being drawn to you like nails to a magnet. Efforts to alleviate anger, stress, anxiety, and confusion—or anything else you'd like to eradicate from your life—also work well now. (The trick is to visualize the problem breaking up into particles that fly away and dissolve into nothingness.)

The good news is that Sun storms are predictable—but only by about three to four days in advance. Still, that allows plenty of time for practitioners to be ready to grab their power and use it to full advantage.

While working with the phases of the Sun can be similar to working with those of the Moon, it's important to remember that He is an entirely different entity. His energies are warmer and simpler in nature, and His properties are direct and to the point. For this reason, you may find that magic performed in harmony with the Sun doesn't necessarily react in the manner to which you've become accustomed. You may find that it hits its mark immediately, or with little or no waiting period. And because of that, it's a really good idea to be extremely specific when working with the Sun; otherwise, you may very well wind up with more than you bargained for. And that's a place you simply don't want to go.

As long as you keep this in mind, though, there are few things as magically rewarding as working with the Sun and His properties. Doing so can not only enrich your personal life, but add a sort of balance to magic that you've never known. That said, I urge you to embrace the warm, happy, and harmonious energies of the Sun. You'll be pleasantly surprised at the visible difference it makes in your attitude, your life, and your magic.

Working with the Days of the Week

As magical practitioners, we know that it's possible for efforts to work regardless of the circumstances. We might not have the right candles. We might not have the right stones. We might not have anything that the initial instructions call for at all, but that doesn't really matter. The fact of the matter is that we can often bring the desired results through nothing but sheer concentration and force of will. Even so, we're always looking for those little extras to boost our efforts and provide the outcome we envision. Why? Because magic is supposed to make our lives easier instead of more difficult. And having those extras on hand can make all the difference.

Knowing when to cast a spell and when not to is one of those little extras. And that knowledge is especially important when it comes to working with the masculine energy of the Sun. The reason is that the Sun's energy is very direct in nature, and magic that incorporates this type of energy often hits its mark much more quickly than we're accustomed to. That means that there's little room for error on the part of the practitioner. More to the point, it means that we must be extremely specific not only with what we want and how we want it, but we must be careful to work in harmony with other energies specific to the task at hand. And knowing which day corresponds to your effort will give you the proper edge.

That being the case, take a little time to familiarize yourself with the following information. It will not only go a long way toward providing the results you want, but will help to prevent anything unexpected.

Daily Influences Chart

Sunday

This day is ruled by the Sun. It provides an excellent energy for efforts involving general gain and success, business partnerships, job promotions, business ventures, and professional success. Magical work involving friendships, joy, and mental or physical health also benefit from this influence.

Monday

Monday belongs to the Moon. Its energy benefits efforts that deal with women, the family, home and hearth, the garden, and medicine. It also boosts rituals involving psychic development and prophetic dreaming.

Tuesday

Mars rules Tuesday. Try it for work involving men, conflict, physical endurance and strength, lust, hunting, sports, and all types of competition. It's also a great tool for rituals that deal with surgical procedures or political ventures.

Wednesday

Wednesday is ruled by Mercury. Its energy is most beneficial to efforts involving writers, poets, actors, teachers, and students. That's because its influences vibrate toward inspiration, communications, the written and spoken word, and all forms of study, learning, and teaching. It also provides a good time to begin efforts that deal with self-improvement or understanding.

Thursday

Jupiter governs Thursday, and influences work that involves material gain, general success, accomplishment, honors and awards, or legal issues. Its energies also benefit matters of luck, gambling, and prosperity.

Friday

Friday belongs to Venus, the goddess of love. Since its energies are warm, sensuous, and fulfilling, it's of great benefit to efforts involving matters of the heart, pleasure, comfort, and luxury. Use it, too, for any magical work that deals with music, the arts, or aromatherapy.

Saturday

Saturn, the planet of Karma, presides over this day. It provides excellent conditions for efforts that involve reincarnation, karmic lessons, the mysteries, and wisdom. Its energies also benefit any work that deals with the elderly, death, or the eradication of pests and disease.

Giving the Sun His Due

Since the Sun rules our week—and literally gives us our days—it's only right that we should give Him some credit. But when incorporating Him in our magical practice and using His powers for gaining what we desire, we need to go a step further than that. We need to thank Him, praise Him, and ask for His blessing. Simply put, we need to give Him His due.

The best way to handle this is through a simple but heartfelt daily devotion. While this devotion doesn't have to be anything fancy or take much time, it's important to do it every morning without fail. Traveling, and don't have the appropriate candles? Not a problem. Just do the devotion anyway, and visualize the candle burning. You'll be amazed at the difference it makes in your day. It's a good bet, in fact, that you'll wonder how you ever managed to get through a day without it.

A sample devotion to the Sun follows on page 77, as do sample devotions to the ruling planets of the individual weekdays. Whether you decide to do the latter or not is strictly up to you. However, spending that extra few minutes on the daily planetary energies is definitely a worthwhile expense. Why? For one thing, the Sun rules the week and all the planets involved—and by paying your respects to them, you inadvertently honor Him as well. For another, it attunes you to the predominant energies of the day and brings blessings that might not ordinarily avail themselves to you. More importantly, though, it helps you to form a firm relationship with the planets, and you'll want that in place should you ever feel the need to call upon them for magical assistance. Remember: there's just no such thing as having too many allies—especially when it comes to magical practice!

As with any other sort of magic, remember that these devotions should reflect your lifestyle and your way of doing things, so don't hesitate to change the wording, incense, or candle colors as you see fit. But since it's important to get the energy of the Sun flowing through your body and spirit, please begin the devotion in the general starting position outlined below. And not to worry if you're physically challenged. Just visualize yourself in the starting position, and go from there.

Daily Devotion to the Sun

Stand with your feet apart and your arms raised even with your shoulders to form a star. With the left palm up and the right palm down, breathe in the grounding energy of the Earth and exhale any scattered energy through your mouth. Continue to breathe in this fashion until you're totally relaxed.

Then call on the Sun, saying something like:

Father Sun, Who turns the night

Into the day with golden light

I give thanks for all You bring:

Warmth, strength, hope, and other things

Like laughter, joy, and true affection

And for holding me in Your protection

I thank You for my life this day

Please bless me with Your golden rays

And with Your wisdom, warm and bright

Please open me unto Your light

Into my body let it swell

Infusing each and every cell

To energize 'til day is done

This I ask you, Father Sun

Repeat the invocation twice more, and stay in the position until you feel the energy begin to swirl through your body. Then light the appropriate incense and candle, and move on to the devotion for the correct day of the week.

Planetary Devotions for Individual Days

Sunday

Planet: Sun

Ruling Angel: Michael[1]

Incense: Frankincense

Candle Color: Yellow

O Glowing Sun of fiery light

I thank You for this day

And for the blessings You bestow

As I go on my way

I ask Your blessings of success

Today, O Mighty Sun

And that your angel, Michael, watch
O'er me 'til day is done

Monday
Planet: Moon
Ruling Angel: Gabriel
Incense: Jasmine
Candle Color: White

O Shimmering Moon of silver light
Please bless me on this day
And send Your angel, Gabriel
To help me on my way
Please lend your strength to all I do
Uncover all deception
Unravel every mystery
Today without exception

Tuesday
Planet: Mars
Ruling Angel: Khamael (sometimes called Samael)
Incense: Cinnamon
Candle Color: Red or orange

O Planet Mars, Who rules all wars
And all sorts of competitions
Please bless me as I live this day
And free my inhibitions
Please send Your angel, Khamael

> *To lend a helping hand*
> *As I reach out for victory*
> *Toward all achievements planned*

Wednesday
Planet: Mercury
Ruling Angel: Raphael
Incense: Nag Champa
Candle Color: Purple

> *O Mercury, of fleeting foot*
> *And flowing inspiration*
> *Please bless me as I work today*
> *And bring cooperation*
> *From Your angel, Raphael*
> *So mental blocks shall cease*
> *Grant fresh perspective now as well*
> *Let ideas flow with ease*

Thursday
Planet: Jupiter
Ruling Angel: Tzadkiel (sometimes called Sachiel)
Incense: Frankincense or cinnamon
Candle Color: Green

> *O Prosperous Planet of Jupiter*
> *Who causes cash to flow*
> *Smile upon me with Your gold*
> *And end financial woe*

Call Your angel, Tzadkiel

And set him to this task:

To aid and guide me toward success

Please do now what I ask

Friday
Planet: Venus
Ruling Angel: Anael (sometimes called Haniel)
Incense: Vanilla or rose
Candle Color: Rose or blue

O Gorgeous Venus, One of love

And One of luxury

Please bring Your blessings to my day

And shower them on me

Please call Your angel, Anael

To guide me through the day

That I may see Your wondrous gifts

As I work and play

Saturday
Planet: Saturn
Ruling Angel: Zaphiel (sometimes called Cassiel)
Incense: Nag Champa or camphor
Candle Color: Black or navy blue

O Teaching Saturn, planet of

All lessons and all trials

Please ease the things I learn today

But make each one worthwhile

And call Your angel, Zaphiel

To stay right at my side

And point out what I may not see

Together, be my guide

Endnote

1. In his book, *The Magus* (originally published in 1801), Francis Barrett lists the Archangels Michael and Raphael interchangeably as ruling the planets of the Sun and Mercury. To avoid confusion, I have listed Michael with the Sun and Raphael with Mercury. For further information, please see the new edition of this book, published by Red Wheel/Weiser, March 2000.

3

Everything Under the Sun

The position of the Sun at birth is an important factor for the magical practitioner. Why? Because it controls the personal intellect and all things psychological. It governs what we, as individuals, think and see, and colors our perceptions of life in general and of the world in which we live. And it's these influences that shape the parts of the psyche that determine who we really are and who we may become.

But what about the personal Moon sign? Since it affects our emotions—and emotion is the catalyst from which all magic stems—isn't that the determining factor when it comes to all things magical?

Well, yes and no. While it's true that the personal Moon sign does govern our emotions and plays a large role in how we feel about the events in our lives, it functions primarily as the fuel that powers the magic at hand. So, it's not the only factor that figures in. The personal Sun sign, on the other hand, acts more like a combination of accelerator pedal and steering wheel. It determines to what degree and how quickly we actually act upon our feelings, how much of what we really think is carried into the outside world, and the manner in which we deliver it. Simply put, it reflects the real person or the ego.

Take me, for example. I'm a Taurus, the eternal Earth Mother and nurturer. This means that no matter how aggravated I am about something—whether mundane or magical—you'll seldom find me *intentionally* handling it in any way that's likely to hurt someone. I also tend to be very slow toward any sort of real action, and do a lot of thinking first. Once I've made up my mind, though, I tend to be quite stubborn when it comes to alternative suggestions. In fact, wild horses couldn't keep me from going through with my original plans—unless, of course, someone's able to prove me wrong in black and white.

So what does this mean magically? It means that while my actual work is slow and methodical—and my magic is usually created with a tender touch—there's absolutely nothing gentle about its delivery. In fact, it soars through the Cosmos with the force of a hurricane. And it's that stubbornness—that unbelievably strong will—of Taurus that makes it come across that way.

With that in mind, it's easy to see that the personal Sun has a lot to do with what is actually expelled into the Cosmos during the spellcasting process. This means that it's more than just a little prudent to work with your Sun sign and understand both its advantages and shortcomings inside and out. Doing so can be a great help in bringing clarity to thought patterns, clearer foresight, and greater success. And when it comes to the magical planning process, there's just no such thing as too much help.

But that's not the only reason to explore your personal Sun sign in conjunction with magical practice. Fact is, the Sun controls the physical realm. It is the planet of here and now. And when we're working toward manifesting something in the physical realm, it's downright silly to ignore the power that rules the very plane upon which we wish to see it materialize. It's the same as throwing perfectly good energy in the trash. And because magic is all about harnessing, moving, and directing energy, that's a place a wise practitioner would never dream of going.

That being the case, do yourself a favor and gather the wisdom at hand. Familiarize yourself with your personal Sun sign and see how it applies to your magic. Once you do, the magical realm won't just become an easier place to navigate, but everything within its boundaries will begin to shine with a clarity you've never known. Guaranteed.

Which Witch is Which?

What follows below is a brief description of each Sun sign and how it handles the magical work that comes its way. "Brief" is the keyword here, though. For more information and further exploration, it's probably a good idea to check out a good book on astrology, read up on your sign, and draw your own conclusions.

It's also important to note that working within the period ruled by your particular Sun sign can bring results more expediently than you ever thought possible. Why? Because you're automatically in tune with that period, since it vibrates to the very strengths that navigate your magic. And that's a little like having a magical co-pilot at the helm during operations. For that reason, you may want to schedule complicated efforts—or their planning sessions—for that time.

Aries Sun Sign

Aries is, without a doubt, the action figure of all Sun signs. There's no such thing as inertia when it comes to this one, and it's never heard the word "lazy." It has a "lead-follow-or-get-the-hell-out-of-the-way" kind of attitude, and pushes forward—even in uncharted territory—with unsurpassed momentum. This means that magical efforts undertaken by this Sun not only fly hard and fast, but bring quick results as well. And that's good news.

The bad news? Because of its pioneering energy—and its need to get something done—Aries often thinks too little and plans too late. And unfortunately, this means that the results originally envisioned aren't always those that materialize.

If Aries is your Sun sign, try the affirmation below. Said on a daily basis, it will go far in counteracting your magical weaknesses and bringing your strengths into focus.

Aries Sun Affirmation

I burn a trail through uncharted space

Action is mine, for great speed is my pace

But even in movement, my mind is a'twirl

With thoughts of the future—how it will unfurl—

With each step in place and each avenue planned

The magic envisioned unfolds by my hand

Taurus Sun Sign

The Taurus Sun sign is that of the Eternal Earth Mother. It cultivates and settles, nurtures and stabilizes. And when it comes to magic, thought and planning aren't a problem for this sign. It looks for the best solution for everyone concerned, and then, using little more than sheer force of will, it catapults the effort right into the Cosmos.

In the case of Taurus, though, the same willful constitution that sets the magic soaring is also its downfall. Why? Because this sign simply will not listen to the suggestions of others or look at alternative measures. And this can mean the difference between a perfectly manifested effort and one that's merely mediocre.

If Taurus is your Sun sign, try the affirmation below. Said on a daily basis, it will help to counteract your stubbornness and bring your strengths into focus.

Taurus Sun Affirmation

I am a settling, nurturing force

I stabilize all as I plot out my course

But I listen to all and I hear what is said

I toss alternative measures around in my head

I sort through the options and choose the best route

So magic will shine from within and without

Gemini Sun Sign

Commonly known as the Great Communicator, Gemini is simply full of ideas and plans. It thinks things through, plans things out, and looks at all the options before setting things in motion. And once it's sure that everything's in order, it sends its magic into the Universe with a creative force unrivaled by any other Sun sign.

So, what's the problem? While Gemini really does do everything right at the outset, it has extreme difficulty with focus. And this means that efforts often fly off helter skelter and occasionally even peter out before hitting the mark at all.

If Gemini is your Sun sign, try the affirmation on the following page. Said on a daily basis, it will help to minimize problems with concentration and bring your strengths into focus.

Gemini Sun Affirmation

> *I bring ideas—I am true inspiration—*
> *I am the magical awe of creation*
> *But with all things magical, focus is key*
> *So I gather my thoughts and I hold them to me*
> *And once they're in order, I set them to flight*
> *So manifestation is strong, clear, and bright*

Cancer Sun Sign

As the Homebody of the Sun signs, Cancer not only creates safe, comfortable space, but nurtures all who enter there. And when it comes to magical navigation, those qualities definitely shine through. What's more, Cancer plans carefully, thinks things through, looks at the big picture, and knows how to concentrate. Once magic is set into motion, it not only flows smoothly into the Universe, but wraps itself around the precise components necessary for proper manifestation.

Since everything's in place for perfectly constructed magic, it's obvious that Cancer's problem has nothing to do with mechanics. The culprit, instead, is a severe distrust in the workings of the Universe. And because this sign isn't absolutely certain that things will work as planned, they seldom do.

If Cancer is your Sun sign, try the affirmation below. Said on a daily basis, it will go far in minimizing your fears and bringing your strengths back to the forefront.

Cancer Sun Affirmation

I am the Magic of hearth and of home

Of safe, sacred space found wherever I roam

My magic is strong and it flows out with ease

Wrapping itself 'round the lands and the seas

Weaving itself into manifestation

And breathing the life of a brand new creation

Leo Sun Sign

As the Great Entertainer of the Sun signs, there's little that Leo likes better than being on stage. And the world of magic provides exactly what it needs most: a captive audience for its grandest feats. In fact, magic constructed by this Sun sign is generally designed to be elaborate and awe-inspiring, as well as thoroughly entertaining, and it's a safe bet that delivery and manifestation will be, too.

The problem is that Leo simply doesn't like inconvenience and aggravation, so anything remotely annoying is likely to be discarded when it comes to magical practice. (Leo just doesn't think all those rules are necessary.) And this can mean the omission of valuable steps toward proper manifestation.

If Leo is your Sun sign, try the affirmation below. Said on a daily basis, it will go a long way toward bringing your strengths to the forefront, and help to minimize any magical weaknesses.

Leo Sun Affirmation

I am the magic of great entertainment

For mine is the joy of creative arrangement

But even so, I must follow the rules

Plotting each step and preparing each tool

So magic will manifest as is the plan

And come to fruition as I know it can

Virgo Sun Sign

I've often heard Virgo called "the button counter of the Universe," and there's no better description. This Sun sign is definitely the Prime Organizer, and you'll never find any other practitioner so perfectly structured when it comes to magic. All the i's are dotted, all the t's are crossed, and every single rule—even those that others might find obscure—are followed with absolute precision. Of course, magical navigation and manifestation follow suit—for no effort delivered at the hands of Virgo would dare to materialize in any other fashion than the one originally specified.

For all its good points, though, Virgo has real trouble adapting when things go awry. And since the magical world isn't perfect, it's often necessary to flex and flux and change plans in midstream to stay on course. This Sun sign simply isn't built that way, so its magic often just stays on the altar, sitting and waiting until Virgo collects itself and gets with the program.

If Virgo is your Sun sign, try the affirmation below. Said on a daily basis, it will do much to maximize your magical strengths and counteract any manifestation weaknesses.

Virgo Sun Affirmation

I organize magic with real ease and grace
All is in order, with all in its place
But when things go awry, I adapt, too
Adjusting my plans so that magic flies true
I learn to pinch hit, and I go with the flow
For magic, like life, isn't always "just so"

Libra Sun Sign

Holding domain over the scales of the zodiac, Libra is the Great Balancer. It weighs and measures everything, making absolutely sure that it's all meted out equally in the sense of sound judgment and fair play. Such is the case with its magical practice, too. All efforts are constructed so that everyone concerned gets a fair shake. And when it comes to magical navigation and manifestation, there's an even flow of energy unrivaled by any other Sun sign.

The problem is that Libra frequently goes way too far in the weighing and measuring process. So much so, in fact, that it often has extreme difficulty making any sort of a firm decision. There are simply too many variables to consider—especially when it comes to magic. And by the time this Sun sign finally gets around to giving wing to magic, the window of opportunity has already slammed shut.

If Libra is your Sun sign, try the affirmation below. Said on a daily basis, it will go far in making short work of any magical weaknesses and do much to strengthen your manifestation skills.

Libra Sun Affirmation

I am the Balance—I tip and I weigh
The magical steps in my efforts as they
All come together in one structured plan
But when all is ready, I find that I am
Ready to act and I set magic free
For I am the Magic and the Magic is Me

Scorpio Sun Sign

Commonly known as the Occultist of the zodiac, there's no other Sun sign quite as seductive as Scorpio. That's because this Sun sign is magic personified. There's nothing it can't uncover, nothing it can't accomplish, and nothing it can't manifest. And once Scorpio has an effort in place, it not only flies straight to its mark, but seems to manifest nearly before the final words are spoken. There's no other Sun sign who can boast that.

Like every other Sun sign, though, Scorpio has its magical drawbacks. The most significant drawback is that Scorpio is way too emotional for its own good. And instead of realizing this and corralling the energy a bit, this Sun sign uses every smidgen to back its magic and send it soaring into the Universe. The result is anything but pretty. In fact, the magic often manifests in such uncontrollable ways that even Scorpio can't manage it.

If Scorpio is your Sun sign, try the following affirmation. Said on a daily basis, it will go a long way toward strengthening your manifestation skills and dissolving any magical weaknesses.

Scorpio Sun Affirmation

I am the Occultist—I am the Magician—
But within magic, I break my tradition
Of building and building the power inside
Instead I direct it so that it won't slide
Out of control and cause magical stress
I shape my results and how they manifest

Sagittarius Sun Sign

As the Traveling Philosopher of the Sun signs, Sagittarius questions absolutely everything. And this is good news when it comes to magical operations, for it means that this sign isn't likely to leave any stones unturned in the process. It knows what it wants and it knows how to make it happen. Even better, it knows how to navigate the Universe with such a straight path that manifestations are likely to come both on target and with ease.

There is a problem, however, when the questioning mind of Sagittarius simply refuses to stop. It begins to wonder if the magic will work, what will make it work, and what will happen if it doesn't. Before it's said and done, Sagittarius has picked the entire operation to shreds, and come to believe that the magic didn't really work at all. (Any sign that it's working, of course, is nothing more than a figment of the imagination.) This is nothing short of magical self-sabotage.

If Sagittarius is your Sun sign, try the affirmation below. Said on a daily basis, it will bring your magical strengths to the forefront, and go far toward counteracting any weaknesses in personal manifestation skills.

Sagittarius Sun Affirmation

Mine is the question, for I am the Sleuth

I find the answers that uncover truth

But in my search for the facts, I know, as well

That my magic works; all such fears are dispelled

My questions are silenced as it comes to be

For I am the Magic—the Magic is me

Capricorn Sun Sign

Because of its practical, pragmatic nature—and its persistent insistence that things be done just so—Capricorn is often known as the Jewish Mother of the Sun signs. Laugh if you will, but these are the very characteristics that make its magic so effective. It doesn't have a problem engineering the most complex operation, and even understands the need to occasionally switch gears enroute. Regardless of the situation, Capricorn can come up with a practical solution. And when it materializes on the physical plane, you can bet your bottom dollar that the manifestation itself will reflect that practical air as well.

The problem is that this Sun sign simply refuses to look at any alternative measures whatsoever—even if it's obvious that things are headed in the wrong direction. That's because Capricorn truly believes that its way is the only way. (Anything else, of course, is bound to fall short.) This means that Capricorn often misses the mark and winds up having to deal with messes of its own creation—messes that could have been avoided if it just hadn't been too stubborn to consider other lines of thought.

If Capricorn is your Sun sign, try the affirmation below. Said on a daily basis, it will go a long way toward strengthening your manifestation skills and relieving any weaknesses that hinder results.

Capricorn Sun Affirmation

> *I am the pragmatic and practical Sun*
> *But I understand that no test can be won*
> *Without seeing options and looking anew*
> *At other ideas, other thoughts, or fresh views*
> *And armed with revitalized strength and the rest*
> *I am at the peak of my magical best*

Aquarius Sun Sign

Known as the General Contractor of the Sun signs, Aquarius has a knack for finding weak spots and problem areas, and removing them without a trace. But its real talent lies in the areas of restoration and reconstruction skills, for this Sun sign can rebuild, reform, and reshape at the drop of a hat. Those are very valuable skills, indeed, when it comes to the magical process. Why? Because even if something goes awry, Aquarius can fix it, restore it, and send it on its way. And that's exactly why efforts undertaken by this Sun sign always seem to manifest with ease.

As good as that is, though, a problem occurs occasionally for Aquarius. And that's because it seldom looks past the end of its own nose before introducing magic. It forgets to look at the big picture and what's at stake. It's that failure to see things in the larger scheme that brings an onslaught of self-induced problems that Aquarius will eventually have to handle.

If Aquarius is your Sun sign, try the affirmation below. Said on a daily basis, it will bring your magical strengths into focus, and go far in counteracting any weaknesses that hinder your results.

Aquarius Sun Affirmation

I restore and reshape everything in my sight
And bring it new strength and fresh luster, so bright
But I see the whole picture before I begin
To find the true nature of what should have been
And determine how my work will affect the whole
For a sound reconstruction will now be my goal

Pisces Sun Sign

Just as the other Sun signs, Pisces plays an important role in the astrological scheme: in short, it acts as the Universal Conscience. With its sensitive nature, gentle sense of compassion, and constant flow of fresh perspective, this Sun sign works hard to keep us in line. And its magic definitely reflects that. For this reason, efforts undertaken by Pisces generally flow through the navigational channels with ease and manifest in a gentle, fluid motion.

Since there's obviously no difficulty with magical mechanics or specs, what's the problem? Nothing more than a simple lack of self-confidence and self-esteem. Because of the gentle nature of its magical process, Pisces seldom realizes that the effort at hand is not only working, but already beginning to materialize. And as a result, it thinks the effort was for naught. Instead of actually looking to see what's happening, it just curls into a ball of misery and resolves itself to not being good enough, smart enough, or talented enough. It's magical sabotage at its worst.

If Pisces is your Sun sign, try the following affirmation. Said on a daily basis, it will help counteract any poor self-esteem and self-confidence issues and bring your strengths back into focus.

Pisces Sun Affirmation

I am the Power, the Magic, the Key
All that I touch reflects each of these
My magic is strong—each effort flows true—
I see clear results in all that I do
I trust in myself, for I am the Key
The Power, The Magic: I am all three

The Birth Day

Even though the position of the Sun at our birth has a lot to do with our navigation and manifestation, there's something else that factors in magically, too. It's something that we seldom think about, but something just as important. Instead of governing how we navigate and manifest magic, though, it deals with the types of efforts that come easily to us, talents that we're born with, certain inherent magical abilities, and, occasionally, even a physical attribute or two. And that something is the day of the week on which we're born.

Most of us don't give this so much as a second thought. But that's probably not our fault. So much is written about astrology, the position of the planets at our birth and how they affect our lives, that the birth day just gets lost in the shuffle. We forget that the planets also rule the individual days of the week and that their energies comprise very specific gifts bestowed upon their chosen. In fact, such was probably the impetus for the nursery rhyme of unknown origin that follows below:

Monday's child is fair of face
Tuesday's child is full of grace
Wednesday's child is filled with woe
Thursday's child has far to go
Friday's child is loving and giving
Saturday's child works hard for a living
But the child who's born on the Sabbath day
Is fair and wise and good and gay

Of course, this doesn't mean that every child who's born on Wednesday is absolutely miserable, or that all children born on Sunday are positively wonderful. Such is certainly not the case. However, there is a shred of truth in each one of the statements above, albeit somewhat skewed. And that's something we'll take a look at as we go through the individual days.

But there's more to this line of thinking than some worn-out nursery rhyme. Much more. Knowing what your specialties are will give you an opportunity to develop them. Knowing what your talents are will give you the chance to use them. And knowing where your inherent magical abilities lie will open your world to limitless possibilities. So, take a moment to determine the day of the week you were born, and let's get started.

Sunday

This day is ruled by the Sun, and since it begins our week, it's a very important day, indeed. The Sunday-born generally enjoy a sunny disposition, but most are marked by that sparkling, fluid smile that seems to wrap all the way around their faces. But there's more to being born on this day than meets the eye. Why? Because the Sun holds dominion over the week as a whole. And this means that all of the planetary energies involved in the week belong, at least in some small way, to you. With that in mind, I can't think of any reason at all why someone born on a Sunday could ever be less than "fair and wise and happy and gay." Can you?

Magically speaking, those born on Sunday wind up with two very special gifts: those of success and illumination. And though these seem to touch every effort worthy of their time, they are especially helpful when it comes to divination by crystal-gazing and working with the chakras. The Sunday-born also excel in efforts that involve business partnerships and ventures, professional success and promotion, and general prosperity, as well as those where joy, friendship, or mental or physical health are an issue.

Monday

Monday belongs to the Moon, and the energy She extends to Her children is nothing short of magical. While the Monday-born receive this gift in many different ways, they often carry the Moon's radiance by way of a flawless complexion and a round face. (They also tend to retain water and go through occasional emotional upheaval as the Moon grows to full.)[1] They are usually characterized by their mischievous eyes and silvery voices that flow like silk. And even though it's probably not their intention, they seem to shroud themselves in a veil of mystery that even the Sun Himself couldn't melt through. Perhaps it's because of this that Monday's child seems to have a knack for working behind the scenes and drawing everything together, while everyone else seems frozen in place.

Magically speaking, the Monday-born seem to have a true affinity for the cup, for working with the Water Element, and for all things liquid and fluid. Most of them possess an inherent ability for prophecy and divination, an eye for deception, and a real talent for empathy, as well. But that's not all. Those born on Monday also excel in efforts that involve women, home and hearth, the family, the garden, travel, and medicine, as well as rituals designed to boost psychic development and prophetic dreaming.

Tuesday

Mars rules Tuesday. And though His gifts are definitely magical, they are, for the most part, geared toward living well in the mundane world. He generally gifts the Tuesday-born with some sort of athletic ability, whether it be a knack for hopscotch, or something more grueling, such as a career in gymnastics, track and field, or hockey. Since most Tuesday-born also possess the grace, agility, and rhythm of a warrior, they make excellent dancers and can choreograph anything. Add Mars' exceptional grasp of hand-to-eye coordination, and it's doubtful you'll ever find an even remotely clumsy Tuesday's child—much less any who could manage to fall over their own two feet.

But what about talents in the magical realm? Well, there are plenty of those for the Tuesday-born, too. In fact, they have an exceptional eye for planning magical strategies and resolving problem areas in spells and rituals. Efforts that involve political ventures or politicians, and those concerned with conflict or competition are definitely within their forte. They also excel at efforts related to physical endurance and strength, sports, hunting, war, sex and lust, and those involving surgical procedures.

Wednesday

Wednesday is ruled by Mercury. Although He claims many wonderful attributes—speed, agility, and so forth —He's best known for His sense of creative genius. And that's usually the gift He imparts to His children in some way, shape, or form. Ideas don't just flow for the Wednesday-born, though. They seem to pop out of nowhere. And they don't just come a few at a time, either. They come at a rate so fast and furious that it's nothing short of mind-boggling to the rest of us. If that's the case, then what's up with this "full of woe" stuff? Well, if you had so many ideas that you couldn't possibly act on all of them, wouldn't you be more than a little aggravated? I sure would!

Wednesday's child also carries this gift of creative genius into the magical world. And there, it usually presents itself in the form of the written word. This means that the Wednesday-born are generally pros when it comes to writing rituals, spells, and incantations, and that their Books of Shadows are probably the most complete you've ever seen. They also excel at any efforts that involve inspiration, communications, writers, poets, the written and spoken word, and all matters of study, learning, and teaching. But that's not all. They're masters when it comes to rituals related to self-improvement or understanding.

Thursday

Having a reputation for being the happy, jolly sort, Jupiter presides over Thursday. But while His children generally enjoy good moods, that happy-go-lucky attitude isn't all He imparts to them. Physically speaking, they usually have a stout bone structure. Their faces often enjoy nice, tight little apples in the cheeks, and eyes that crinkle away to nothingness when they laugh. And why shouldn't they? Jupiter doesn't just bestow the gift of wealth upon Thursday-born—He also leaves them the tools to keep the prosperity coming. All of this is hard work, however. And in order to work to potential, Thursday's child does, indeed, "have far to go."

From a magical perspective, the Thursday-born are drawn to metal tools such as the athame and pentacle, and work well with the Earth Element. And drawing from the physical potential for wealth, it only stands to reason that their ritual specialty is that of material gain. If that's not enough, they also excel at efforts involving general success, accomplishment, honors and awards, or legal issues. And they simply can't be beat when it comes to those matters concerning luck, gambling, and prosperity.

Friday

Friday belongs to Venus, and She wraps Her children in that warm, sensuous, fulfilling energy of beauty that only She exudes. As such, the Friday-born at least appear to be aesthetically beautiful, even if they really aren't. They usually have striking features—haunting eyes and full, sensual mouths—often softened by dimples. Friday's children are also usually gifted with some artistic ability. But even if they're not, they love beautiful things. They have an exceptional eye for color, composition, and texture, and know how to make it all work together. (The latter is so true, in fact, it's doubtful that a tasteless or tacky Friday's child has ever even existed!) If that's not enough, Venus also gifts Her children with loving hearts and a generous spirit. What could be better than that?

Magically speaking, Friday's child is a born gatherer. These people always have a full assortment of interesting tools and supplies, and are never caught lacking in ritual. They are often quite talented in the arts of incense and oil-making as well. The Friday-born excel at efforts that involve any type of pleasure, comfort, and luxury, as well as the arts, music, or aroma. But because of the sensual gifts of Venus, their real specialty lies in matters of the heart.

Saturday

Often described as the "Pulse of Nature" and lending His name to the last day of the week, Saturn presides over Saturday. And the gifts He brings His children are great, indeed. While some of them are bestowed with strong, willowy frames, a larger portion enjoy a sort of physical fluid motion and body flexibility that most other people can't boast. But their most striking feature usually has to do with the changeability of their faces. They never seem to look the same way twice; in fact, it would appear that they're born shapeshifters. Because of Saturn's agricultural nature, though, His gifts don't stop there. He also imparts the Saturday-born with a love of growing things and an inherent interest in plant life. And this often culminates in occupations like farming or flower arrangement, and hobbies such as gardening—all hard, dirty work.

Born herbalists, the Saturday-born not only have a knack for identifying plants, but for mixing them into wonderful tinctures, potions, washes, and powders of the magical sort. And because their specialty is reincarnation and its lessons, they frequently make good past-life regressionists. They also excel at efforts involving the mysteries, wisdom, the elderly, death (real or symbolic), long-term projects, and the eradication of pests and disease.

Endnote

1. In some cases, the removal of silver jewelry can counteract the problem. For more serious cases, however, medical attention may be necessary.

4

Solar Illumination

When it comes to performing monthly rituals—the sort that invite particular influences into our lives—the Moon is usually at the forefront. That's because we're conditioned to see the Moon as the purveyor of magic, the source of our power, and often, the catalyst from which our magic springs.

Most of us never even give the Sun a second thought. And that's a tragedy, indeed. Why? Because the position of the Sun is important to magical practice, too. It determines the energies that are inherently present as the Sun moves from one astrological sign to another. And taking advantage of those energies can make all the difference when it comes to magical success.

Take the period of April 20 through May 20, for example. Ruled by Taurus, it's a very fertile period, indeed. The Earth seems to green overnight, flowers burst into full bloom, and animals everywhere busy themselves with the reproduction process. Now, couple that with the fact that Beltane and either the Hare or Dyad

Moon come into play during this period, and you have a veritable fertility extravaganza on your hands.

Invoke the energies of the Moon during this time, and you definitely level the odds for magical success. But invoke the Sun as well, and a real transformation is in the works. Suddenly, this energy isn't just something you can feel or see. It's something you can touch, and smell, and hear. It becomes something so tangible that it goes past any realm of human consciousness. It becomes a real part of your being, coursing through every part of your anatomy, until at last you become the energy itself. And when you become the energy, your magic can't help but take flight and come to fruition posthaste.

Be that as it may, most practitioners completely ignore the Sun and His astrological journey. They forget to give Him equal time. And in doing so, they set themselves up for magical mediocrity. More importantly, though, they miss out on specific energies that could make the personal world an easier place to live—a place where clarity is key and personal success abounds.

That having been said, do yourself a favor. Include the Sun in your monthly rituals, and ask Him to infuse you with His energies. The difference it makes in both your life and your magic will not only be immediate, but will exceed your wildest expectations.

For your convenience, a generic Sun ritual is included below. Use it as a guideline, and change it to suit your individual lifestyle and preferences. Remember: the more you personalize a ritual, the better the results. And results are what you're after!

General Sun Energy Invocation Ritual

(For best results, perform this ritual on the first day of the Sun's astrological change, or the first Sunday thereafter.)

Start by cleansing your body, your mind, and the ritual area just as you normally would for any other formal Circle. Place the Element symbols at the appropriate Quarters, and use your regular altar setup for incense placement and ritual tool arrangements. The only difference between setting up for this ritual and any other is that the altar candle—which is usually white—should be replaced with one of a bright yellow, gold, or yellow-orange hue to honor the Sun. (Candles in a color appropriate to specific Sun sign energy may be added if you wish. For further information and celebration ideas, see the individual Sun Celebration sections that follow.)

Light the candles and incense, purify and cast the Circle, and call the Watchtower Guardians to guard, protect, and witness the ritual. Move to the center of the Circle, ground and center, then say something like:

This is a place not a place
In a time not a time
This Circle is sealed

> *By the words of this rhyme*
> *And floating in balance*
> *'Twixt both worlds this day*
> *I worship the Sun*
> *And due homage I pay*

Wait a couple of heartbeats, then stand with your legs apart and your arms aloft. Invite the Sun into the ritual by saying something like:

> *Father Sun, Who brings the Day*
> *Who guides us with His shining rays*
> *Who bathes us in His light so warm*
> *Whose rainbows signal end of storm*
> *Who wakes the seed so that it grows*
> *Who brings good health and ends our woes*
> *Who smiles on us and brings success*
> *And fills our hearts with happiness*
> *With every loving touch He gives*
> *Unto this plane on which we live*
> *Please descend now from above*
> *And touch this Circle with Your love*
> *Please join us in this sacred rite*
> *O Father, bring Your love and light*

Wait a few moments until you feel His presence, then recite the Charge of the God[1] in His honor:

I am the echo you hear in the forest, deep

And the warmth of the Sun upon your face

I am the ageless sound of the ocean's roar

And the power that's felt in every wild place

I am the wheat that rustles low on the breezes

And the spark that ignites the hearth fire

I am the passion and power and ecstasy

That is reached at the end of desire

I am the squirrel who plays games in the treetops

And the young stag who runs wild and free

I am the clatter of hooves on an old gravel road

And the strength of the ancient oak tree

I am found in the wrinkles of the old crippled man

I am found in the child, young and strong

I am found in the joy of the union of love

In the passionate kiss, slow and long

I am your Lover, your Father, the Ancient One.

Take my hand and I'll teach you the Dance

Of the change of the seasons and the eye of the storm

Of fertility, love, and romance

Remember always, my children, be merry

Hear the lilt of my music, so light

And hold sacred My realm and all it sustains

As you dance to My tune in the night

Wait two heartbeats, then ask the Sun to fill your Spirit with the energy of the astrological sign at hand, and help you to understand its lessons. For your convenience a general invocation follows below. (For invocation ideas appropriate to specific Sun energies, see the individual Sun Celebration sections that follow.)

O Fiery Father, Who art Sun

O Spark of all Creation

Please grace me with Your presence now

Accept my invitation

Infuse me with Your brilliant Light

As Your Mysteries I embrace

I ask You, Father, come to me

Descend upon this space

After the invocation, perform any magical work you had in mind. When you're done, hold the cakes in front of you and bless them by saying something like:

I conjure You, O Meal of Grain

Who sprouted in both Sun and Rain

Whose ancient seed fulfills us all

And gains new life where e'er it falls

I bless You in this Circle round

That Your abundance may abound

And feed our world continuously

As I will, so mote it be

Eat one of the cakes. If this is a group ritual, take a bite, then pass the platter to the person on your left with a kiss and a "Blessed be" or a "May you never hunger." When the platter reaches the altar again, proceed with the wine or juice blessing by holding the liquid in front of you and saying something like:

I conjure You, O Fruit of Vine

Who grew with Wind and Rain and time

From nothing but the light of Sun

And light of Moon when day was done

I bless You in this Circle round

That Your abundance may abound

And feed our world continuously

As I will, so mote it be

Pour the liquid into a goblet and take a sip. If this is a group ritual, pass the goblet to the person on your left with a kiss and a "Blessed be" or a "May you never thirst." When the goblet reaches the altar again, you can either take some time to visit with each other in Circle, or proceed with closing the ritual. Should you choose the latter, thank Father Sun for attending the ritual by saying something like:

Father Sun, Who brings the Day

Who guides us with His shining rays

Who bathes us in His light so warm

Whose rainbows signal end of storm

Who wakes the seed so that it grows

Who brings good health and ends our woes

Who smiles on us and brings success

And fills our hearts with happiness

With every loving touch He gives

Unto this plane on which we live

We thank You for Your presence here

And hold You in our hearts so dear

And with our love now, You may go

Or stay, if You should deem it so

Dismiss the Guardians and release the Circle. Then go outdoors and leave some cakes and wine for the animals.

That's all well and fine. But what if you're just not into formal ritual? What if you're a more laid back sort of person who sees nothing at all celebratory about that kind of pomp and circumstance? What then?

Not to worry. Just have a party!

Because the Sun's energies focus on what's happening in the physical realm more than any other planet's energies do—and because the Sun positively radiates warmth and joy—nothing could be more appropriate. Just start the affair with a toast appropriate to His current astrological position, and include other activities designed to honor Him. (Specific toasts and ideas follow in the individual Sun Celebration Party Ideas sections.) Most importantly, though, plan your party with the idea of having fun. Since Sun energy is an exuberant sort that resonates to laughter and merriment, no real Sun celebration would be complete without it!

Sun Celebrations

Sun in Aries (March 20–April 19)

Thematic Energy: Of all the signs through which the Sun journeys, Aries reigns supreme when it comes to astrological moving and shaking. It just can't help itself. After all, it's ruled by Mars, the planet of action and war. For this reason, it's also considered to be the pioneering sign—the sign that forges ahead through uncharted territory, breaking through barriers and exploring regions that no other sign would touch with a ten-foot pole. It is, for all practical purposes, the prime initiating force.

With that in mind, the period during which the Sun moves through Aries couldn't be more appropriate. Why? Because Mother Nature is also forging ahead, breaking new ground, and getting things done. She not only has to tend to seed germination and root system formation, but see to it that the tender new sprouts are strong enough to push their way through the Earth. She has to conjure enough wind, rain, and light for everything to work. That's not all, though. She's also busy prodding the animals in Her keep to reproduce and repopulate. Mother Nature is, indeed, at Her most active just now—and there's not a second to lose!

Mundane Energy: Since Aries provides a "let's get it done" sort of energy, anything that requires tying up loose ends is a good bet now. Finish projects, clean up that junk room, or get rid of those clothes you haven't been able to wear for a year. Since it's also a good time for preventative maintenance and replacement measures, give your car the once-over. Check the wipers, belts, and tires. Change the oil and schedule an appointment for a tune-up. Do a complete check of your house, too. Paint, tend to the new weather stripping, and buy new appliances, if necessary. And because all this costs money, pick up the phone and call in old debts—there's no better time for successful collection—and enter some contests that tout cash prizes. Job applications seem to meet with much success now, too. But if you already have the job of your dreams, go for the gold and ask for that raise. You have nothing to lose—not with the warm rays of Aries on your back and guiding you forward!

Magical Energy: Since action is key when working with this sign, nearly anything that requires moving ahead is a good candidate for magical efforts. Work on fresh starts and new opportunities. Issues that involve jobs and promotions, prosperity, and health also come into play. Got issues that you'd normally save for the

Waning Moon? This is a good time to handle those as well. Work efforts to assist you in removing yourself from that damaging relationship, or ripping depression and bad habits from your life. But that's not all. Because this sign is ruled by Mars, there's no better time to work on issues that relate to soldiers and war, personal battles, victories, challenges, accomplishments, and personal success. Use this period as well to bless and consecrate all ritual tools and supplies that involve the Fire Element. (Athames, censors, candles, incense, and matches come to mind here.)

Because the Ostara celebration may coincide with this period, and the rising of either the Seed or Hare Moon—or both—occur now as well, other magical possibilities are at the forefront, too. If the Ostara energy is present, use it to fertilize and add oomph to workings that may prove complicated or difficult. If the Seed Moon rises during this period, incorporate Her energy by taking some time to consecrate your garden space and gardening tools, and, of course, the seeds you wish to plant. If, on the other hand, the Hare Moon's in residence, anything that involves fertility—pregnancy, the addition of new characteristics in your life, the creation of a new business, and so on—can't help but meet with success as well.

Aries Sun Circle Sample Invocation

O Pioneering Spirit of the Great Aries Sun

Great Mover and Shaker of boundaries won

Come into our hearts, our minds, and our souls

Lending Your power as we reach toward our goals

Shedding Your light as we sift and we dredge

Through possibility waiting for us on the edge

Of opportunities lurking in boundaries unclaimed

Help us discover that which we can attain

Aries Sun Circle Ideas

- Dress in shades of red and orange to welcome the Aries Sun.

- Use red candles on the altar, and burn Aries incense. (To make your own incense, use a mixture of cinnamon, galangal, juniper, and rose petals.)

- Decorate the altar with symbols that represent movement and the pioneering spirit. Good ideas might include pictures of magical pioneers such as Gerald Gardner or Alex Sanders, or historical pioneers such as Amelia Earhardt, Albert Einstein, Sacajewea, or Ben Franklin. Maps and small exploration tools such as hand shovels and picks also work well, as do artistic prints that show movement (color photocopies of Van Gogh's paintings come to mind here).

- Mark the Circle boundary with shoes to symbolize movement and action.

• Serve cinnamon bread and spiced red wine for libation. (For a non-alcoholic beverage, try spiced cider.)

Aries Sun Party Ideas

• Decorate with the colors and items suggested in the Circle Ideas section.

• Serve chili pie, nachos, or something equally spicy to honor the fiery nature of the Aries Sun.

• Serve each attendee a Tequila Sunrise. (Please see the Celebratory Drink appendix for recipe.) For non-alcoholic drinks, serve cider or orange-cinnamon tea. Then offer a toast to the Sun by saying something like:

Here's to the Aries Sun, so dear

Who now burns in the sky as the Great Pioneer

Who beckons us onward as we forge ahead

Exploring, discovering, and staking our stead

Taking due action as onward we run

Here's to the light of the new Aries Sun

• Tell stories of your favorite magical, historical, or ancestral pioneers, and how their dedication to exploration impacted your life. Let everyone have a turn.

• Write the names of well-known pioneers on slips of paper, and give one name to each attendee. Ask each person to give a few clues as to his or her "identity," then let the others guess who they are. Let everyone have a turn.

- Small bags of cinnamon candies make excellent party favors. Make tags with a set of footprints on one side and the phrase "Always move forward" on the other. Tie them to the bags.

Sun in Taurus (April 20–May 20)

Thematic Energy: Once Aries has cleared the way, Taurus moves in to settle, develop, and cultivate. There's nothing shoddy about the way Taurus settles in, though. Ruled by Venus, this Sun sign simply exudes refinement, so when it's in charge of the building and construction process, you not only can count on long-term stability, but bet your bottom dollar that luxury, comfort, pleasure, and abundance will come into play as well. Couple that with its Venusian love of romance and fun, and there's no better choice for the new world's master developer.

During this time, Mother Nature is well-ensconced in the construction business, too. She builds upon the Aries period sprouts, and brings them to new life with Her strength. They grow tall and green, strong and vibrant. They bud and blossom with Her fertile artistry, filling the air around us with heady perfumes and sensual beauty. Then She goes one step further by delivering the newborn offspring of our animal siblings—and presto!—the Earth has been transformed right before our eyes. It's the most splendid garden and wildlife preserve we've ever seen, and we have Mother Nature to thank for our lovely new home.

Mundane Energy: We already know that Taurus energy is all about the development and cultivation of that which makes us comfortable. So it should come as no surprise that the period it rules is an excellent time to buy a home, start building the one you've been planning, or remodel the one you already have. You're perfectly happy with your home and its floor plan? Then spruce it up a bit. Paint the walls that scrumptious color you've always dreamed of, redecorate with new wallpaper, or invest in new furniture. (Think comfort and luxury when you shop, but don't forget to pick up the important things that will secure your home from harm. New locks, batteries for the smoke alarms, or updated security systems come to mind here.) Since Taurus brings the arts, pleasure, and romance to the forefront as well, it's also a good time to get out and about. Dance, accept party invitations, go on blind dates, or start a love affair. And who could forget about the Taurean urge to hoard cash? That being the case, spend some time planning your financial future. Open bank accounts, reorganize your finances, or work on stock portfolios. And above all, don't forget to check around for that perfect retirement plan. Bullish Taurus would never be caught without plenty of cash—and you shouldn't be, either!

Magical Energy: Since Taurus easily builds on that which is already present and develops that which isn't, the sky's the limit on what can be accomplished here. Efforts that involve becoming more comfortable with oneself, such as self-esteem or self-confidence, are good options, as are any issues that relate to inner strength or self-empowerment. Because this energy also lends itself to work related to security, stability, and protection, it also provides a good time for protective blessings of all types—homes, pets, children, belongings, theft prevention, and any other magical work that involves your personal environment or surroundings. Need cash? Then this is the perfect time to work on that, as well. I've never seen any prosperity spell fall flat when performed in conjunction with the green energies of Taurus.

The Beltane celebration occurs during this period, too, and brings with it an energy so fertile that it's unsurpassed by any other. This is great news for those who wish to work on matters of the heart, for there's nothing else like it to boost efforts involving love and romance, and those related to long-term goals like marriage. (Careful with this energy, though; otherwise, pregnancy could also become an issue!)

And if the occurrence of Beltane weren't enough to fertilize any magical effort you have in mind, try this on for size: the Hare and/or Dyad Moon also come to fullness now. Should it be the Hare Moon, use its energies to add special oomph to any and all magical efforts. If the Dyad Moon rises instead, harness those energies for complicated works—especially those involving relationships.

Taurus Sun Sample Invocation

Come to us, Taurus—we welcome Your light

We ask that You fertilize all in our sight

Help us to build on and stabilize, too

The plans we develop—the work that we do—

And lend to our spirits Your rich dedication

To love and romance; be our inspiration

To cultivate all that is good in our lives

Bring Your warmth to us, Taurus, and help us to thrive

Taurus Sun Circle Ideas

- Dress in shades of green and rose to welcome the Taurus Sun.

- Use green candles on the altar, and burn Taurus incense. (To make your own incense, use a mixture of amber resin, patchouli, musk, vetivert, jasmine, and sage.)

- Decorate the altar with symbols that represent growth, fertility, construction, and stability. Good ideas might include cut flowers in full bloom or small potted plants to symbolize Mother Nature's fertile development and cultivation process. For a more worldly type of altar, try pictures of the early settlers, bridges and fences, or well-cultivated Shakespearean knot gardens.

- Mark the Circle boundary with the flowers and greenery to symbolize the fertile cultivation of the Earth.

- Serve butter cookies and mimosas (champagne mixed with orange juice) for libation. (For a non-alcoholic beverage, try milk laced with honey and vanilla extract.)

Taurus Sun Party Ideas

- Decorate with the colors and items suggested in the Circle Ideas section.

- Serve something creamy and substantial for this party. Stroganoff, cream soups, and cheesecake come to mind here.

- Serve each attendee a Golden Dream. (Please see the Celebratory Drink appendix for recipe.) For non-alcoholic drinks, serve frappe (ginger ale poured over sherbet), then offer a toast to the Sun by saying something like:

Here's to the stability of the great Taurus Sun

Who settles and cultivates the boundaries we've won

Whose romantic nature and sensual style

Brings comfort and luxury, making us smile

As we build and develop and fertilize, too

Here's to You, Taurus, and all that You do

- Hold a fundraiser of sorts with the money going to a favorite charity. One fun idea is to "auction off" the party attendees with the "prize" being some personal service they're willing to offer. This could be a day of housework, a tarot reading, natal chart, or numerology report, or even a day of errand-running.

- Ask everyone to bring some fresh-cut flowers—even wildflowers will do—and spend some time arranging them into tiny bouquets. Tie them with brightly-colored ribbons and deliver them as a group to a nursing home or hospital. (For bouquets that deliver their own messages, provide a book on floriography and make tussie mussies instead.)

- Small bundles of fertilizer sticks tied with green ribbons and blessed for growth and stability make excellent party favors.

Sun in Gemini (May 21–June 21)

Thematic Energy: Now that Taurus has provided us with comfortable surroundings, it's time to get on with the business of living. But with so much to do, it's hard to decide just where to begin. Fortunately for us, Gemini comes to the rescue, and with its appearance, opens the lines of communication. Ruled by Mercury, messages flow fast and free. We talk to each other, share ideas, and examine new angles. We discuss plans, set them to paper, and come up with solutions. But it doesn't stop there. We also learn about each other, what makes us tick, and how we can best utilize our talents for the good of all. It's all a part of the communication process. And nobody handles that better than Gemini.

Mother Nature steps in kind, for the rest of Her world is busy communicating, too. The warmth of the Sun beckons us forth to bask in its light, while branches laden with leaves promise the cool respite of shade. Enticing us with their beauty and fragrance, flowers simply beg to be picked. But that's not all. With Mother Nature voicing Her demands with perfect clarity, animals lose their winter coats. Birds teach their young to fly. Young predator animals learn to hunt. Even the bees are busy, buzzing about and combining their efforts toward the coming honey harvest. And it's all because they've made a connection—a connection so static-free that even the most subtle of messages can get through.

Mundane Energy: Because this period is all about communications, now is the time to write, write, write! In fact, there's no better time to take care of paperwork or tend to those projects that involve paper and pen. Sign contracts, work on proposals, or write that speech or article you've been putting off. Need to answer letters? Now is the time to do it. With the energy of Gemini at the forefront, you can be sure that every word will hit its mark and nothing will be misconstrued.

But the written word isn't the only thing that works well now. This is an excellent time to voice new ideas and perceptions to business associates and those in authority. Plans for trips and detail-oriented projects tend to go off without a hitch, too, and if that's not enough, the expansive energies of Gemini also provide the perfect atmosphere for upgrading all your communications devices. So, if you've been waiting to update or replace your computer, peripherals, telephones, or other electronic devices, wait no longer. Check the sales papers and head for the store. Deals are typically good at this time of the year, and you may even be able to talk your way into a discounted service contract or two!

Magical Energy: Since magic simply can't come to fruition without solid communication between the worlds, this particular period is an important one. This is especially true when working with efforts that require any sort of expansion. (Business ventures, matters of the heart, or other rituals that you would normally perform during the Waxing or Full Moon come to mind here.) It's also excellent for writing rituals and working on matters that involve inspiration, creativity, and inventiveness. Have a problem that needs a quick magical resolution? Give it a shot now. Gemini has a way of clearing things up in short order, so there will never be a better time to handle it. And because of the airy nature of the period, don't forget to use this energy in the blessings and consecrations of wands, incense, and garden windsocks, as well as those for personal vehicles such as cars and boats.

With this period may also come the harvest festival of Midsummer, and if that's the case, you'll want to take full advantage. How? By communicating with the fairy-folk and fey, of course. It's the best time of the year to engage them to do your bidding, and their help can be priceless in all things magical. However, know that you must offer them something in return and make good on your promise; otherwise, they tend to get ornery and may toss more than just a bit of mischief in your direction, and that's something you can certainly do without.

This sign also plays host to either the Dyad or Mead/Honey Moon. Should the Dyad Moon guest at this time, use its energies to sort through complicated matters, especially those involving love. If the Mead/Honey Moon comes to call, though, its energies are better used as a catalyst toward magical efforts that involve metamorphosis or transformation.

Gemini Sun Sample Invocation

Come to us, Gemini—Communicative Sun

Who expands all horizons with words He has spun

We ask that You bring us new thoughts and perception

Grant our voices be heard with the warmest reception

And let that which we speak hit its mark loud and clear

So it's not misconstrued and it meets with no fear

Help us sort through our problems and those, expedite

Inspire us, O Gemini, with the warmth of Your light

Gemini Sun Circle Ideas

• Dress in shades of yellow and cream to welcome the Gemini Sun.

• Use yellow candles on the altar, and burn Gemini incense. (To make your own incense, use a mixture of violet petals, lavender, cinnamon, thyme, myrtle, and heliotrope or sunflower.)

• Decorate the altar with letters, words, and other symbols of communication. Try spelling out the phrase "Light our way," "Welcome Sun," or some other Sun-related phrase with alphabetic building blocks. Other ideas might include an arrangement of quill pens and inkwells, sheet music, an alphabet garland, or even several floriography-related flower arrangements.

• Make a chain from strips of paper upon which qualities you'd like to include in your life have been written, then use it to outline the Circle boundary.

• Serve lemonade and sugar cookies for libation.

Gemini Sun Party Ideas

• Decorate with the colors and items suggested in the Circle Ideas section.

• If you're planning a dinner party, try rotisserie chicken and augratin potatoes. If this is more of a party where refreshments are served, go with lemon pound cake or lemon sugar cookies and lemonade.

- Serve each attendee an Orange Blossom. (Please see the Celebratory Drink appendix for recipe.) For non-alcoholic drinks, serve lemonade. Then offer a toast to the Sun by saying something like:

  Here's to the Expander—the Gemini Sun

  Whose eloquent skills bring us together as one

  Whose letters and words, Whose language and rhyme

  Help us sort through our problems in minimal time

  And expand our ideas—fleshing out every thought—

  Here's to you Gemini, and the blessings You've wrought

- Treat your guests to a game of Scrabble, Pictionary, or charades—or, better yet, a contest. Just divide the attendees into teams and let them work together. That way, everyone gets a turn, and all your guests are involved. Give a small prize to the winners.

- Other word games are great for this party, too. Just write phrases on slips of paper and place them in a small basket. Have the first participant draw two slips: one to begin his or her sentence, and one to end it. Then ask the next person to draw one slip. He or she must begin a sentence with the ending phrase of the last person, and end it with the phrase on his or her slip. Continue around until all the slips in the basket are used.

- Inexpensive quill pens and small bottles of ink make excellent party favors. Failing that, try brightly-colored notepads and decorative pencils.

Sun in Cancer (June 22–July 22)

Thematic Energy: We've explored and settled and learned to communicate. And while that's quite an accomplishment, we can't rest on our laurels just yet. Why? Because Cancer presents us with another mission: it's time to tame the wild vestiges and nurture what we've wrought. As such, we find ourselves staking claims, refining our living spaces, and making them our own. That's not all, though. We also begin to turn inward and take stock of what really makes us tick. We realize that love and compassion are necessary factors in true civilization, and with that in mind, we undertake a valuable but transformative lesson—that of learning how to really live, both together and by ourselves. Growth and improvement come to the forefront, but we temper them with the nurturing spirit of Cancer, transforming not only those around us, but ourselves as well.

We're not the only ones in the midst of transformation, though. Cicadas and butterflies burst forth from shells and cocoons. Honey—once nothing more than nectar from early flowers—is ready for the harvest. Flowers and herbs are at the peak of their growing season. And much of the animal kingdom, having just given birth, is now adjusting to the rigors of parenthood. They're not only learning what it takes to bring their young to adulthood, but learning to do it with a sort of instinctual nurturance they've never before experienced.

Mundane Energy: "Home sweet home" is a catch-phrase often associated with Cancer energy, and nothing could be more appropriate. Why? Because this period is all about personal space and sanctuary—at least on a mundane level. That being the case, it's an excellent time to look for new living quarters—quarters that reflect your personal tastes—or reclaim the space you already have. If the latter is more feasible, start by getting rid of the stuff you no longer want or need. Then only add things that reflect your personality, are self-nurturing, and tell the world that this space is yours. Haven't checked your water-related devices in a while? Now's the time to do that, too. Check pipes, fix leaks, and replace faulty spigot washers. It's also a good time to buy sprinklers and garden hoses.

But personal space issues aren't the only things that Cancer energy brings to the plate. This energy is also about long-term plans and goals that affect our living space. Looking for a roommate? Now's the time to place the ad. Involved in an intimate relationship and ready to take things to the next level? I can't think of a better time to propose marriage or seal a long-term commitment. Weddings and handfastings are a good bet now, too.

Magical Energy: Since the taming energy of Cancer is at the forefront now—and this includes home and hearth—it provides a perfect time to create sacred space. So, if you don't already have a special place set aside for magical workings, now is the time to do something about it. It's also a good time to consecrate your altar and magical tools, and bless any water for future efforts. But because home is a sacred space, too, this period is also excellent for related cleansings, wardings, and protection projects, as well as for blessing the stock of food items in the pantry, refrigerator, or freezer. Need to work on some personal issues? Personal growth, self-empowerment, forgiveness, and any work related to curbing emotions is a good bet now, as is anything that involves personal goal-setting.

Should this period bring the festival of Midsummer, a little weather-witching may be in order. It's especially helpful for water-related problems like bringing rain to drought-ridden areas and drying up flood waters in those overly-saturated areas. One word of caution, though: codicil your weather workings with a request that water not be taken from another drought area or returned to one that's already too wet. The idea here is to solve problems—not to create them!

Either the Mead/Honey Moon or the Wort Moon will come to call at this time as well. Should the Mead/Honey Moon rise, use its energies toward efforts that involve personal transformation, a complete reinvention of your life, or a change in personal reality. If Cancer brings the Wort Moon, though, try its energies for work that involves psychic development, meditation, or inner-journey work.

Cancer Sun Sample Invocation

Come to us, Cancer—O Nurturing One—
Lend us direction 'neath the light of Your Sun
Show us the way as safe space we do fashion
Guide our emotions and bring us compassion
Lend us Your power as we set our goals
Whether mundane or magical; and as we play our roles
Within this world, in the Cosmos, and life
Shine on us, Cancer, with Your rays gold and bright

Cancer Sun Circle Ideas

- Dress in white or cream to welcome the Cancer Sun.

- Use white candles on the altar, and burn Cancer incense. (To make your own incense, use a mixture of camphor, musk, and clove.)

- Decorate the altar with a collection of stained-glass suncatchers, crystal prisms, or other objects designed to reflect light into the home. Other ideas might include an arrangement of sunflowers, marigolds, or other yellow and orange flowers to honor the Sun.

- Since the Water Element belongs to Cancer, you may want to go further than simply mixing it with a little sea salt and using it to asperge the Circle. In fact, outlining the Circle boundaries with water-related objects—sea shells, or watering cans or vases filled with flowers—can be fun.

- Serve white wine or flavored water and lemon cookies for libation.

Cancer Sun Party Ideas

- Decorate with the colors and items suggested in the Circle Ideas section.

- This is the perfect time for an ice cream social, but if you choose to go that route, do it up right by having several topping flavors on hand. For a dinner party, serve shrimp or crab salad with ranch dressing, or seafood gumbo and white wine. If snacks are more to your liking, though, crackers and chips with crab dip will work well.

- Serve each attendee a Bahama Mama. (Please see the Celebratory Drink appendix for recipe.) For non-alcoholic drinks, serve ice water to which you've added lemon slices. Then offer a toast to the Sun by saying something like:

Here's to the Tamer: the Great Cancer Sun
Of the home and the hearth—the Nurturing One
Who creates sacred space and Who harvests us all
Whose warmth and Whose light both relax and enthrall
Who brings forth true feeling in all that we do
We honor You, Cancer, with this toast to You!

- Since this period is about nurturing and transformation, have the attendees sit in a circle and, working in a clockwise fashion, take turns saying something complimentary to the person on their left. You'll be amazed at how it changes everyone's attitude and leaves them feeling both nurtured and pampered.

- Other ideas for this party might include water-related sports. Don't have a swimming pool? No problem. The local public pool, the seashore, or your favorite swimming hole are viable options. Failing that, have a water gun contest with the object being to wash a spot of shaving cream from a target while blindfolded. Give a small prize to the winner.

- Small seashells blessed for home protection make great party favors.

Sun in Leo (July 23–August 22)

Thematic Energy: Now that we've come to terms with our surroundings and tamed the inner self, it's time to go out and play, and the Leo Sun begs us to do just that. It doesn't have to twist our arms, though, since we know it's time for a break. We've worked hard, and we deserve a little fun. But Leo beckons us way beyond that. It brings on the urge to entertain— to take center stage—and to throw one hell of a party. That being the case, we find ourselves turning outward once again, meeting new people, visiting with the neighbors, and socializing more. We look up old friends and reestablish those relationships as

well. It's all about fun, festivities, and impromptu celebration—and nothing achieves that better than the
golden warmth of the joyful Leo Sun.

But what about Nature? How does the Leo Sun
figure in there? Well, it's harvest time, and nearly
every crop—from herbs to grains to those deep within
the personal core—is ready for the picking. And
even though there's work to be done, there's also a
real sense of accomplishment at not only managing
to manifest a successful crop—that's quite a feat, in
and of itself—but in bringing it in on time. We've
been blessed with more than we ever hoped to imagine, and I can't think of a better reason for a party!
Can you?

Mundane Energy: From a mundane standpoint, we already know that the Leo Sun brings entertainment,
celebration, and parties to the forefront, but that's
not all. It's also a great time to join groups, widen
that circle of friends, and form new relationships.
(Don't discount the possibility of taking that current
relationship to the next level, either, for Leo also
provides the perfect atmosphere for that.) Been
wanting to try your hand at acting or public speaking? Now's the time to sign up for that drama or
speech class and make your way to center stage.
Plagued with a shy demeanor or a lack of self-confidence? Not to worry. Leo has a way of giving all in his
grasp that much-needed shot of courage, so right
now, there's no problem with stating your needs or

standing up for yourself. One word of caution, though: remember to be tactful. When Leo energy comes to call, diplomacy often flies out the window.

This is also a great time to plan a small getaway, or take that vacation. Why? Because this energy is not just about having fun; it's also about you. And when you combine the two, you just can't help but have an absolutely fabulous time. So, decide where you'd like to go and make the arrangements, then pack your bags and prepare for the adventure of a lifetime!

Magical Energy: Since the Leo Sun brings fun and entertainment back into our lives, now is a great time to perform those fabulous rituals you wrote while under the influence of Gemini. You'll not only enjoy performing them, but the melodramatic air that comes with this energy is simply wonderful for getting rituals off the ground. (You'll find that it's really easy to hone in on visualization skills right now, as well.) And because the focus is also on you and your needs, anything concerning the self—self-expression, self-confidence, self-esteem, and self-devotion come to mind here—is a good bet, too. You may even want to consider a complete reinvention of life as you know it. With the Sun riding high in Leo, your only magical limitations are those that you impose.

Because this period also brings the harvest festival of Lammas, it's a good time to take stock of what you've accomplished and what's still left on your plate. Then take steps toward any goals you haven't achieved and structure magical workings toward their success and manifestation. I've also discovered that the Lammas period is just lucky in general. So, if you're a gambler, this could be a good time to bless any funds you plan to use toward that end.

Should the Wort Moon rise during this period, use its energy toward working with the fruits of your personal spiritual harvest; that is, cementing the relationship you've cultivated with the deities, taking newly-developed divinatory skills a step further, or using any freshly altered perceptions and attitudes toward your spiritual advancement. If the Barley Moon should rise instead, its energy is better used outside yourself. This means that your relationships involving others—those that have to do with love and romance, finances, friendships, general success, opportunities, and so forth—are better bets right now.

Leo Sun Sample Invocation

We invoke You now, Leo—O Great, Shining One
Show us the way by the light of Your Sun
Help us to visualize that which we need
So we reach our goals with the greatest of speed
Squelch our inertia with Your motivation
Teach us empowerment through transformation
Guide us in playing our roles on Life's stage
We welcome You, Leo, as Your warmth we engage

Leo Sun Circle Ideas

- Dress in shades of yellow and gold to welcome the Leo Sun.

- Use yellow and gold candles on the altar, and burn Leo incense. (To make your own incense, use a mixture of frankincense, musk, lemon, patchouli, balm of gilead, and rose petals.)

- Decorate the altar with fruits, vegetables, grains, and flowers of the season. Symbols of the participants' accomplishments work well, too, and these may be in the form of pictures or words as space will allow.

- Line the Circle boundary with scattered thyme and rosemary to imbue the area with joy, and cast the Circle using a single sunflower tied with a gold or yellow ribbon.

- Serve lemonade and sugar cookies for libation.

- Use this Circle to praise and entertain the Ancients. Just ask each participant to invite his or her personal deities into the Circle by calling Their names out loud, and then say something complimentary about the Deity evoked when Its presence is felt. Remember to thank each Deity for personal blessings (go ahead and list them, for the Ancients love that), and ask for His or Her blessings on the group as a whole.

Leo Sun Party Ideas

- Decorate with the colors and items suggested in the Circle Ideas section.

- This is the perfect time for an old-fashioned cookout or barbeque. Just provide the entrée and drinks—sun tea or lemonade—and ask each attendee to bring his or her favorite dish. If you're concerned about having too many salads, desserts, or whatever, provide a sign-up sheet several days prior to the party.

- Serve each attendee a Frozen Sunrise Margarita. (Please see the Celebratory Drink appendix for recipe.) For non-alcoholic drinks, serve lemonade or orange juice. Then offer a toast to the Sun by saying something like:

  We praise You, O Leo, the Great Shining Sun

  Who helps us to reach toward accomplishments won

  Who brings possibility to knock at the door

  And helps us to see what we could not before:

  That we are the Divine—that It lives well inside

  Here's to You, Leo! High may You ride!

- Since this Sun is all about showing off, have an impromptu talent show. This not only gives attendees license to take center stage, but will provide hours of fun for everyone. Offer a small prize to all participants. (With so much talent, it might be hard to decide upon a winner!)

- Group sing-a-longs can be a fun avenue to take with this kind of party, as well. Don't worry if you don't have a piano or don't play an instrument well enough to accompany others, just provide a karaoke machine and let the fun begin!

- Lemon or orange lollipops make excellent party favors. Just use a magic marker to draw a picture of the Sun on the plastic wrappers, and tie the stems with yellow and orange ribbons.

Sun in Virgo (August 23–September 22)

Thematic Energy: Now that we've taken a well-deserved break to enjoy Leo's fabulous stage show, it's time to roll up our sleeves and get out the brooms, mops, and garbage bags. That's right. We have to clean up the mess that's always left behind after a good party. And fortunately, that's exactly the sort of energy the Virgo Sun brings with His arrival. We suddenly feel the need to straighten things up and put them in order. But since fleet-footed Mercury rules this Sun, the here and now really isn't at the forefront on this one. We're looking ahead, knowing full well that we're eventually going to need certain bits of information right at our fingertips. And if we don't organize it now, we'll never be able to find this stuff when we need it. So, we're doing what we can to make sure that life runs smoothly a little farther down the road.

All of Nature is planning ahead, as well. The harvest period is in full swing, and grain-crop remnants are quietly reseeding into the Earth so they'll be ready for Spring sprouting. Squirrels and chipmunks busy themselves with the initial stages of nut collection. Even the trees are busy. With the dormant period just around the corner, their leaves change color and prepare to fall so that none of the nutrients necessary for good root health are wasted during the Winter months.

Mundane Energy: When the Virgo Sun comes to call, there's no time to waste. It's time to put things in order and get organized. Got a messy desk? Now's the time to clean it up! Haven't balanced your checkbook in a while? Virgo won't let you rest until you get it done! In fact, now is not only the time to get busy with everything on your to-do list, but to put things in order so that your very life is a more efficient process. Since this may involve a little shopping on your part—especially if you simply don't have any place to put your stuff—see what you've got and decide upon the best way to organize it. Then check out the sales ads for plastic bins with snap-on lids, divided desk organizers, bookcases, and so forth.

But organizational skills aren't the only thing this Sun provides. It also brings a good time to schedule all those things you've been putting off, so make that appointment with the doctor or dentist, or schedule that surgery, if need be. Delve into contracts, make necessary changes, and sign on the dotted line. Check your portfolio to see whether or not additional financial planning is in order. Been meaning to talk to your favorite charity about some volunteer work? Now is the time to make the call. It's also the time to think about future plans, especially those that require your commitment, so give them some thought, then make decisions based on the best outcome for all involved.

Magical Energy: There's nothing like the Virgo Sun to help us put our ducks in a row—and this is true magically, as well. Since the procrastination phase has come to a screeching halt, this is the best time ever to get busy with your Book of Shadows. Plan it, organize it, and include all those things you've been meaning to add. In short, tie up those loose ends—or papers, as the case may be—and put things in order so they're easy to find when you need them. Been meaning to take care of a particular situation magically, but just haven't gotten around to it? Now is the time to do it. This is also a great time to perform efforts that involve finance, future plans, or any sort of productivity or structure. Don't discount this energy, either, for efforts involving traditional values. Whether they concern romance, family, or the workplace, Virgo can make them happen.

If this period brings the Fall Equinox festival of Mabon, issues of connectivity are at the forefront. And this provides an excellent time to look at who you are, where you're going, and who you want to become. Other connections are important, too, so you may also find yourself looking at your links to other people and the interactions involved. Only you can determine whether these associations need improvement or are best completely severed, but either way, there's no better time to handle those issues.

Should the Barley Moon rise during this period, use its energy for efforts that involve health, family, and personal well-being. Those efforts that require a strengthening of sorts—whether a relationship matter, an issue of self-confidence or courage, or something involving finances—work well now, too. If the Wine/Harvest Moon rises instead, its energy is better used in areas of study, knowledge retention, meditation, and astral projection. It's also very beneficial in increasing divinatory and psychic skills.

Virgo Sun Sample Invocation

We welcome You, Virgo—You Who organize—
Lend, please, Your structure to each enterprise
That we undertake now so that all falls in place
Bring new commitment as our work we embrace
Teach us of ethics, of values, and morals
Shed light on the problems of resting on laurels
And help us to plan for our futures as well
Come to us, Virgo! By Your light we excel!

Virgo Sun Circle Ideas

- Dress in shades of orange, gold, and tan to welcome the Virgo Sun.

- Use orange and gold candles on the altar, and burn Virgo incense. (To make your own incense, use a mixture of lavender, wintergreen, orris root, and rose petals.)

- Since simplification and organization are key during this Sun, don't use anything on the altar that isn't absolutely necessary. If you feel the need to decorate anyway, go with a single flower or stem of grain in a bud vase.

- Because this period concerns itself with tying up loose ends, line the Circle boundary with lengths of ribbon tied together in bows. Then cast the Circle with an organizational tool of some type. (A ruler or yardstick tied with orange and gold ribbons works well for this.)

- Serve white wine or flavored water, and oatmeal cookies for libation.

Virgo Sun Party Ideas

- Keep decorations to a minimum for this party. A few simple vases of flowers or an Autumn centerpiece will do the trick.

- This type of party calls for a real potluck, so ask the attendees to bring their leftovers. Then have everybody join in by making salads, casseroles, or something else from the items at hand. Make it a "bring-your-own-drinks" party, and all you'll have to provide are dishes, kitchen utensils, and ice.

- Serve each attendee a Long Island Iced Tea. (Please see the Celebratory Drink appendix for recipe.) For non-alcoholic drinks, serve iced tea with a lemon and mint garnish. Then offer a toast to the Sun by saying something like:

Here's to You, Virgo, the Great Organizing
Sun, and we toast to the strength of Your rising
As You help us to sort and You help us to plan
As You help us to finally be what we can
Here's to the impact of Your brilliant rays
As You lead us toward structure in Your special way

- Have a scrapbooking party. Just have each attendee bring a memory book, mementoes, and a smattering of other supplies to be shared among the group. (You supply the colored markers, scissors, and glue.) It's a great way to encourage guests to interact with each other—and an even better way to organize those sentimentally valuable items with which we just can't seem to part.

- Six-inch rulers tied with a colored rubber-band "bow" and decorated with a few paper clips make excellent party favors.

Sun in Libra (September 23–October 22)

Thematic Energy: Now that Virgo's finally gotten things into some semblance of order, Libra comes in to balance things out. This is really important stuff. Why? Because a good portion of what most people possess is absolutely useless; in fact, it's usually either broken, worn-out, ugly, or all of the above. If that's the case with you, all that stuff is doing little more than taking up space. Under the discerning eye of Libra, though, it's much easier to get rid of. And because this Sun is ruled by materialistic, luxury-loving Venus, you'll never have to worry about tossing out something valuable, tasteful, or pretty.

Nature is doing its own balancing act now, too. With young predator animals learning to hunt, the old and weak are culled from the herds, making room for those to be born in the Spring. Animals who hibernate during the colder months are starting to eat more, and those who don't are busy with their Winter food storage. The last of the harvest is in now, too. And the Earth—exhausted from the long period of fertile production—is starting to make preparations for a nice, long nap.

Mundane Energy: When the Libra Sun takes to the sky, virtually nothing escapes His sense of fair play or balancing energy. And if you're one of those people who always does things for others but wonder when your turn will come to receive, guess what?! The answer is "Now!"—especially if you've been neglecting yourself and your personal needs. That having been said, grab your wallet and head for the mall. Libra's energy is perfect for selecting a new wardrobe, updating your hairstyle, or getting around to that long overdue makeover. Been thinking about redoing a room or two in your living quarters? Get up and get with it! Under Libra's Venusian influences, you'll not only wind up with something tasteful, luxurious, and elegant, but something you're sure to enjoy for years to come.

But that's not all. This period also provides the perfect time to look at long-range plans and make decisions based upon your best interests, and those of all involved. That being the case, go through important documents—wills, stock portfolios, and so forth—and make any necessary changes. With Libra's sense of fair play at the forefront, take care of any pending legal issues promptly; if a court appearance is necessary, you'll want to schedule it now as well. And since this Sun sign is most romantic of all, don't discount His effectiveness when it comes to first dates or matters of the heart.

Magical Energy: We already know that Libra is the King of Balance and Fair Play, so any efforts that involve or require these attributes—whether they relate to home, career, or some other area of your life—are certainly good bets during this period. And since sound judgment also comes into play, you can expect success in areas related to the legal arena, good decision-making, or self-awareness. Need a break from all that stubborn narrow-mindedness that seems to oppose your best laid plans? Now's the time to work on that as well; in fact, no other sign under the Sun works quite like Libra when it comes to efforts requiring compromise, cooperation, or teamwork. And because of this Sun's Venusian nature, He also provides the perfect time to work on beauty issues, self-empowerment, and romance.

When the Libra Sun shines on the Fall Equinox festival of Mabon, issues of connectivity still come into play: issues that have to do with the big picture and reach far into the future. And this means taking a good, hard look at where you're going, what you hope to accomplish, and what connections and links may still be necessary to get you there. So, use this period to meditate upon your path, and move forward with any messages that come your way.

If the Wine/Harvest Moon rises now, use its energy for efforts that involve striking a balance between the mundane and the spiritual. And this means that any spell performed now—whether it concerns wealth, cooperation, or anything else—should be engineered to manifest both in the mundane and spiritual worlds. Should the Blood Moon rise instead, perform efforts that involve the well-being of plants and animals, and the good health of Mother Earth. Meditations on the cycle of life, death, and rebirth are a good bet, too.

Libra Sun Sample Invocation

Come to us, Libra—Great Balancing One

Bring sound judgment to light with the rays of Your Sun

Teach us of compromise; make us aware

Of what is required to make all outcomes fair

Teach us the difference that teamwork can bring

To attitudes, workloads, and each little thing

And bring, too, Your love and Your joyful romance

As You shine on us, Libra, and our lives You enhance

Libra Sun Circle Ideas

- Dress in shades of blue and teal to welcome the Libra Sun.

- Use blue candles on the altar, and burn Libra incense. (To make your own incense, use a mixture of lavender, cinnamon, and chamomile.)

- Decorate with symbols of weight, measurement, and balance. Ideas might include measuring cups and spoons, measuring tapes, food or postage scales, or maybe even small hand weights.

- Try something different for the Element symbols. Use a ruler for Air, a thermometer for Fire, a small level for Water, and a scale for Earth. Cast the Circle with a ribbon-tied yardstick.

- Serve chocolate chip cookies and orange-cinnamon tea, or coffee spiked with amaretto, for libation.

Libra Sun Party Ideas

- Decorate with the colors and items suggested in the Circle Ideas section.

- Serve "balanced sandwiches" (sandwiches that include something from all the food groups) and milk at this party.

- Serve each attendee a Sundowner. (Please see the Celebratory Drink appendix for recipe.) For non-alcoholic drinks, serve orange-cinnamon tea. Then offer a toast to the Sun by saying something like:

  Hail to You, Libra, O Balancing Sun

  As You lend us sound judgment in wars lost and won

  For Your sense of fair play

  Regarding what's right and wrong

  For Your impartial justice toward both weak and strong

  For Your help in decisions that balance the All

  We toast to You, Libra, as You rise strong and tall

- Ask attendees to bring whatever they no longer need, and have a "swap meet." (Just provide a table for the goodies and let everyone take what they want.) Better yet, make it an all-day affair and hold a joint yard sale. Give the proceeds to a favorite charity.

- Relay races that involve balance—books on the head, an egg in a spoon, and so on—are good bets for this sort of party. Just divide the group into teams, and let the laughter begin. Give small prizes to each person on the winning team.

• Give ribbon-tied measuring spoons or small measuring tapes for party favors.

Sun in Scorpio (October 23–November 21)

Thematic Energy: With Libra's balancing act at an end, it's time to turn inward and explore our emotions—to look at what makes us tick, and to figure out what excites us and what doesn't. And nobody does that better than the steamy Scorpio Sun. That's because this Pluto-ruled Sun has the ability to shake things up, tear things down, and leave us with little more than the bare bones of personal passion, instinct, and intuition. The actual leftovers aren't really as important, though, as how we apply them. In fact, the application itself can mean the difference between personal demise or absolute victory in the months to come.

But we're not the only ones affected by the energy of the Scorpio Sun. It's rutting season for deer. Driven by a basic instinct to procreate, they busy themselves with the mating process. Stripped of their leaves, the trees are bare now, too. Even the plants have withered away, holding nothing but their root balls secretly within the Earth to ready them again for Spring sprouting.

Mundane Energy: I once heard Scorpio described as "the Rambo of the Universe," and there's nothing that fits it better. It's intense, passionate, and stubborn. It has a black and white sort of viewpoint, and never looks at the gray areas in between. Whether we like it or not, the Scorpio Sun brings basal instinct to the surface and tosses it right in front of our noses. And because it's presented in the rawest form possible, we suddenly find lust and sex—and everything else that goes along with them—staring us squarely in the face. That being the case, this period provides an excellent time to take a good, hard look at personal sexual issues: at what turns us on and what doesn't; at what we truly need for total sexual fulfillment; and, of course, at the steps necessary to bring those things about. There's simply no better time to confront these issues and bring them to resolution both within ourselves and with our partners.

But that's not all that Scorpio throws our way. He urges us to dig beneath the surface and find hidden truths in other areas, too. This makes it a good time to get to the bottom of issues hindering progress in the personal arena. (Career and lifestyle come to mind here, as well as general relationship interactions.) Look at the fine print in contracts, challenge interest rates, and find ways to get the most from your creditors. All forms of study are at the forefront, too. So if you've been thinking of taking a class, now's the time to set things in motion.

Magical Energy: Even though Scorpio has a tendency to strip things down to near-nothingness, no other sign under the Sun brings magic to fruition quite like this one. In keeping with His "bare bones" type of energy, though, it's best to rely on the basics when it comes to magic. And this means keeping things simple, and avoiding any frills, flourishes, or extras that might confuse the outcome of what you really want. With that in mind, this is the perfect time for any effort involving occult and metaphysical studies or skills, as well as those efforts related to past lives or karmic issues. Those efforts that concern metamorphosis or transformation, or even uncovering that which is hidden—especially the sources of current problems—meet with success quickly, too. And don't forget about any issues that involve lust. With Scorpio's basal instinct at the forefront, there's no better time to deal with those problems—or to work a little sex magic!

Because the festival of Samhain occurs during this period, we find ourselves looking at the lives of those who have gone before us, how they lived, and what they did to make their mark on the world. And with the birth/death/rebirth cycle looking us squarely in the face, we often have questions and thoughts that we can't reconcile with our current resources. Take a little time to commune with the dead. Since the veil is very thin just now, communications slip easily between the realms, and the chances of resolving related issues are very promising, indeed.

If the Blood Moon rises during this period, take some time to thank those plants, vegetables, and animals who sacrificed themselves that you might live.

You may also want to collect and dry small bones, vegetable and fruit peels, and seeds for magical workings. If the Snow Moon rises instead, work on any issues that you've had on the back burner for a while. Write the appropriate spells, gather your supplies, and do whatever else it takes to get that magic off the ground and soaring toward the Cosmos.

Scorpio Sun Sample Invocation

Come to us, Scorpio—O Sun of Transformation
And bring us Your gift of true illumination
Uncover the hidden that we might explore
That which is true; unlock ancient doors
Which hold information that we need to know
And help us retain it so that we forego
Mistakes that bring sorrow as we move ahead
We welcome You, Scorpio, and the light that You shed

Scorpio Sun Circle Ideas

- Dress in shades of black and navy blue to welcome the Scorpio Sun.

- Use black candles on the altar, and burn Scorpio incense. (To make your own incense, use a mixture of cinnamon, musk, myrrh, vetivert, and lemon.)

- Decorate with magnifying glasses, or metaphysical or occult symbols—tarot cards, runes, stone, herbs—or just ask each participant to bring a symbol of his or her own personal metamorphosis.

- To add to the transformative theme, place a cauldron in the center of the Circle. Add a small fog machine or a little dry ice for a dramatic effect.

- Serve gingerbread and red wine for libation. For a non-alcoholic drink, serve apple juice or hazelnut coffee with cream.

Scorpio Sun Party Ideas

- Decorate with the colors and items suggested in the Circle Ideas section.

- Because Scorpio energies have a way of disclosing the hidden, plan a menu that's in keeping with that theme. Good snack ideas might include stuffed mushrooms, pizza or egg rolls, pigs-in-a-blanket, or small turnovers stuffed with meat or cheese. For a dinner party, you might center a meal around enchiladas, soft tacos, or stuffed pasta.

- Serve each attendee a Northern Sunset. (Please see the Celebratory Drink appendix for recipe.) For non-alcoholic drinks, serve cider or hazelnut coffee with cream. Then offer a toast to the Sun by saying something like:

  Hail to You, Scorpio, O Sun of Transformation

  Accept now our thanks with this toast of libation

  For Your help in uncovering that which we can't see

  And for shedding Your light on the best we can be

  As we're transformed in warmth by the light of Your rays

  We honor You, Scorpio, as You reign through these days

- Go on a scavenger hunt. List items might include objects that can later be used for magical operations, or ritual tools—stones, shells, and sticks and branches for wands come to mind here—or maps, magnifying glasses, keys, and anything else with an exploration and discovery theme.

- Ask each attendee to bring an unpainted ceramic mask, and have a mask painting party. (These masks are inexpensive, and readily available at arts and crafts stores or your local ceramics retailer.) The idea here is to have the partygoers paint their masks to either reflect the person they'd eventually like to become, or the qualities they'd like to bring into their lives. Just supply a few enamel paint pens in different colors. Your attendees will supply the fun.

- Small magnifying glasses tied with black ribbons make excellent party favors.

Sun in Sagittarius (November 22–December 21)

Thematic Energy: After experiencing the stripping energy of Scorpio, nothing could be more welcome than the Jupiter-ruled Sagittarius Sun. That's because it simply exudes joy, prosperity, and success. But there's more to it than that. Because this energy is less restrictive, we now feel the urge to ask lots of questions; further, we expect answers—even if we have to dig them out ourselves. And since the big picture is at the forefront during this period, we find ourselves saying exactly what we think about the long haul, regardless of the opinions of others. It's a period of personal truth, freedom, and joy—and it couldn't come at a better time.

The natural realm is enjoying its freedom, as well. Shelters and food stores are now in place for squirrels, chipmunks, mice, and insects. Hibernating animals have settled in for a long Winter's nap. And the plant world? Most of it is asleep, too. It's all part of the big picture—that period of reenergizing necessary for the busy seasons to come.

Mundane Energy: With free-wheeling Sagittarius taking His place in the sky, the key phrase is "question everything." And that's exactly what you'll find yourself doing. The search for a personal sense of logic is on, and nothing—not even the proverbial brick wall—can stop you now. At this point, in fact, you won't care what it takes to get what you need, even if it means a series of debates and arguments. You've got enough sense to know that the truth isn't the same for everyone; all that's important is that you find your own. And once you do, you may even surprise yourself with the candid manner in which you express your opinions. The biggest surprise, though, will probably come with the realization that you simply don't care what other people think. You are who you are. Plain and simple.

The good news is that all communications hit their marks with ease now. That means that even if others don't agree with you, your opinions have staying power. In fact, they'll be pondered long after they've rolled off your tongue. So, if you've been meaning to ask for a raise or check into career advancement, now's the time to do it. It's also the perfect time to share ideas and launch plans for the future. But since everything seems up for debate now, make sure you've done your homework. Know where restrictions lie, and be ready with plans to get around them. The only drawback to this energy is that remarks made now are often less than tactful. Just remember that you're much more likely to get what you want if you make a concerted effort to be diplomatic.

Magical Energy: With the Sagittarius Sun casting His light in the magical arena, nearly any effort performed now has the ability to hit its mark. And that's good news. But because of the intensely fiery nature of this Sun, magic often manifests more quickly than originally planned. Of course, this isn't bad news at all; it just means that we have to plan carefully, and be prepared to deal with the results when they arrive. That having been said, work on issues that involve cutting to the chase, unearthing truth, and getting to the heart of matters that have proven to be personal stumbling blocks. Efforts that involve fresh perspectives, new ideas, logic, and philosophies work well now, too, especially when related to long-term plans and goals. But that's not all. Sagittarius also excels in knocking down obstacles, bringing personal freedom, and honing communication skills. And with His true-to-the-mark energy at hand, there's no better time for blessing pendulums and other divinatory devices.

Should the Yule festival occur during this period, rid yourself of any personal character flaws or bad habits once and for all by asking the Old Sun to take them with Him to His death. And with the freshly born Sun starting life anew, it's a great time to ask His assistance in illuminating the source of current problems, and casting light on the most appropriate solutions. His assistance is also unsurpassed in efforts that involve fresh starts, inspiration, and the advancement of projects, both old and new.

If the Snow Moon rises now, use its energies to work on matters related to sleep issues and prophetic dreaming. If no such issues exist, then simply use this period to relax, recoup, and regroup. Should the Oak Moon rise instead, work on matters that involve any sort of balance—especially those that concern balance between the physical and spiritual worlds.

Sagittarius Sun Sample Invocation

Come, Sagittarius—Inquisitive One
Bring fresh perspective with the rays of Your Sun

Help us to question and sort through replies
To cut to the chase—find the truth and the lies—
To see what is useless, what's old and worn out
And bring forth the changes that must come about
For the world to be better for all who live here
We welcome You, Sag, with our love and great cheer

Sagittarius Sun Circle Ideas

- Dress in shades of red and burgundy to welcome the Sagittarius Sun.

- Use red or burgundy candles on the altar, and burn Sagittarius incense. (To make your own incense, use a mixture of pine, musk, myrrh, and juniper.)

- Since Sagittarius is known for hitting its mark, a medieval "Robin Hood" theme can be fun for this Circle. If you choose to go that route, decorate with small bull's-eye targets, bows, and arrows. Another good idea might include decorating with the forest men from the Lego castle collections.

- Wrap and tie an arrow with ribbons in shades of red, and use it to asperge and cast the Circle.

- Serve spiced cider, or spiced red wine, and spice cake for libation.

Sagittarius Sun Party Ideas

- Decorate with the colors and items suggested in the Circle Ideas section.

- Serve chili, stew, or vegetable soup with hot buttered rolls or cornbread, and put coffee, tea, and soda on the beverage menu.

- Serve each attendee a Sunlight Sipper. (Please see the Celebratory Drink appendix for recipe.) For non-alcoholic drinks, serve spiced cider. Then offer a toast to the Sun by saying something like:

  O Sag, Wild Adventurer—Hitter of Marks—

  Whose arrows fly true with a flurry of sparks

  Who gets answers to questions by stirring things up

  And changes the truths upon which we sup

  Who brings new perspective to all that we do

  Sagittarius Sun, we give thanks to You

- This sort of energy is perfect for a costume party. Just ask attendees to dress as their favorite historical, movie, or book character. Set aside time for a question/answer period, and let your guests guess the identity of each character represented. Give a small prize to whomever gets the most right.

- Darts and other bull's-eye games are great fun at this kind of party. But since this event is likely to be held indoors, you might want to use darts with suction-cupped ends, or a game set that's magnetized. (A more grown-up version of Pin the Tail on the Donkey might be fun, too.) Give a small prize to the winning team.

- Give each attendee a forest man from the Legos castle collection as a party favor. (These come with several pieces in a box, are inexpensive, and are readily available anywhere that toys are sold.)

Sun in Capricorn (December 22–January 19)

Thematic Energy: Now that we've discovered our own truths, the Capricorn Sun sweeps in to show us what to do with all that newfound knowledge. And the lessons are just beginning. Under Saturn-ruled Capricorn, we learn about self-discipline and all it entails. We learn about power. But most of all, we learn about practical measures, common sense, and something else that we as human beings all like to ignore: acceptance. Yes, no matter how we slice it, things are what they are, and whether we like it or not, there's nothing we can do to change them at their source.

Predators in the animal world don't seem to have as much trouble with these lessons as we do, but perhaps that's because they're driven by basic instinct and already have a sense of practicality. They know when they're hungry. They know their place in the food chain. But most importantly, they know—and accept—that something else must be sacrificed so they can survive. And while these are Capricorn's lessons in the rawest form, we can learn a lot from taking a good, hard look at them.

Mundane Energy: When the Capricorn Sun illuminates
our world, He also sheds light on personal power issues. We find ourselves looking at how much we have
and how much we give away. More importantly,
though, we find ourselves looking at *why* we give our
power away, and what we need to do to get it back.
Luckily, Capricorn doesn't leave us hanging on this
one—at least not entirely. While it's up to us to figure out the "why," He makes the "what" perfectly
clear: self-discipline brings power, and it's only
through hard work—and a concerted effort to tend
to our own needs—that we can hope to regain what
we've lost.

That being the case, the focus for this period is
practicality. And since frills and other cushy non-
sense have no place here, this calls for taking a good
look at what's necessary and what isn't. It's time to
get down to brass tacks, see things for what they are,
and take charge of our lives once and for all. For
most of us, this means cutting costs, wasting less—
time and money both come into play here—and
learning to make the most of what we've already got.
For others, this may mean a complete reinvention of
life as they know it. Either way it's sliced, one thing's
for sure: we'll eventually be called upon to help others with these lessons. And when that time comes,
we'll definitely know what we're talking about.

Magical Energy: With the practical nature of Capricorn in the spotlight, it's time look at things as they really are. And nothing could be more important magically. Why? Because practitioners can't work to full potential until they've cleaned up their own messes—and Capricorn makes us do just that. Simply put, He urges us to look at our problems and square them away so we can come into our own with a renewed sense of personal power. For some of us, this means working on financial matters. For others, it might involve matters of the heart, issues involving hearth and home, or a simple reclaiming of the energy necessary for personal productivity. Wherever the problems lie, though—even if they require a total lifestyle makeover—now is the time to handle them. Since learning, teaching, and self-discipline top the list of Capricorn's inherent qualities, now is the time to handle any issues involving them, too.

If the Yule festival occurs during this period, ask the dying Sun to help you tie up loose ends, break bad habits, or remove anything unsavory from your life. Ask the assistance of the newborn Sun to shed light on your personal path, to direct you toward its personal lessons, and to offer guidance as you travel. In fact, I'd suggest incorporating the energy of the New Sun in all magical operations just now. Because His light and energy gets stronger every day, it can't help but bring that to your magic.

If the Oak Moon rises during this period, work on issues of strength, courage, dedication, commitment, and personal growth, as well as those that involve physical health, tenacity, and endurance. Should the Storm Moon light the sky instead, use its energies toward efforts related to wishes, awards, and your innermost dreams.

Capricorn Sun Sample Invocation

Come to us, Capricorn—Practical Sun

Help us to see now what needs to be done

To make our lives better; and we ask that you teach

Us of self-discipline so that we may reach

Both the goals in our view and the ones further out

So we may help others bring Your changes about

And help us to see that things are what they are

We honor You, Capricorn—O Practical Star

Capricorn Sun Circle Ideas

- Dress in shades of lavender, plum, and purple to welcome the Capricorn Sun.

- Use purple candles on the altar, and burn Capricorn incense. (To make your own incense, use a mixture of valerian, pine, ylang ylang, and wisteria.)

- Decorate with goal-oriented or knowledge-related symbols—blank certificates of award, blue ribbons, text books, blank report cards, or pictures that depict the goals of the participants—as space allows.

- Use small cardboard posters for Element symbols as follows: a question mark for Air, a light bulb for Fire, an exclamation point for Water, and a graduation cap for Earth.

- Serve granola bars and apple wine or spiced cider for libation.

Capricorn Sun Party Ideas

- Decorate with the colors and items suggested in the Circle Ideas section.

- Provide a platter of cold cuts, cheeses, condiments, and bread, and let guests build their own sandwiches. Trays of deviled eggs, and veggies with dip work well, too.

- Serve each attendee an Amaretto Sour. (Please see the Celebratory Drink appendix for recipe.) For non-alcoholic drinks, serve spiced cider or orange-cinnamon tea. Then offer a toast to the Sun by saying something like:

    O Capricorn Sun, this toast is to You

    For Your lessons, Your teachings, and all that You do

    For the reality checks that You dole out with pleasure

    And Your common sense tactics that we've come to treasure

    For proving that power and gain is all right

    We honor You, Capricorn, and toast to Your light

- Games that involve questions, answers, and thought are perfect for this sort of party, so drag out the Trivial Pursuit, Pictionary, Jeopardy, or Password game. Give small prizes to the winners.

- Competitions of any sort are good bets for this party, too, as long as there's a time limit to make them more challenging. You might, for example, hide several items on the premises and provide clues for the search, allowing a twenty minute timeframe. Just divide the guests into several teams and turn them loose. Give small prizes to those on the winning team.

- Because Capricorn is also mindful of personal gain— and knows how to get it—just tie five pennies in a green cloth and give the bags as party favors. Include instructions to scatter the pennies in the yard for prosperity.

Sun in Aquarius (January 20–February 18)

Thematic Energy: When the Aquarius Sun comes to call, it's time to expect the unexpected. Tradition and protocol seem to fly out the window. Worn-out notions do, too. And the things that fly out of your mouth? Well, no one will be more surprised than you! Not to fret, though. It's just Uranus-ruled Aquarius doing His thing. And while the lessons this Sun doles out— those of individuality and personal assertion—may be hard-earned, He won't leave you hanging. In fact,

He'll not only leave you with everything you need to reshape the personal world into one you can truly live in, but will offer the instructions to boot.

All of Nature is getting a makeover, too. Weather is unpredictable and storms come intermittently. Temperatures rise and fall and snow gives way to rain, but the slush freezes over again and blankets the Earth with ice. For all practical purposes, the world appears to be little more than a slippery, icy, hazardous mess. Beneath the surface, though, some wonderful things are happening; so wonderful, in fact, that some might call them miraculous. The plant world not only lives and breathes, but sleeps soundly beneath that insulating blanket we find so dangerous.

Mundane Energy: To say that the appearance of this Sun shakes things up is putting it mildly. In fact, you may feel that the world as you know it has been positively obliterated. That's because the Aquarian Sun takes His job seriously, and He's busy knocking things down—even things that have always given you comfort—and putting them back together into a more perfect form. Do yourself a favor, and just stand back, relax, and let things play out. Understand that everything's going to be a little off-kilter for a while, and there's nothing you can do about it.

In the meantime, do a little reconstruction of your own. Take a look at what you really want and what you really need. Think about what you really believe, who you really are, and who you hope to become. Spend some time thinking about what hinders your progress, then weed it from your life immediately and irrevocably. Plagued with old projects that didn't work out the first time? Pull them out. With Aquarius shining brightly overhead, all problems come to light. You'll be back on track in no time. This is also a great time to rearrange rooms and work with energy flow in the home, so get out the feng shui books and get busy. And while you're rearranging, remember that something of yours should figure prominently in each room. This period is about you. And that's exactly what your home—and your life— should reflect.

Magical Energy: With the Aquarian Sun cutting through restrictions and bringing freedom to the forefront, now is the time to spread your magical wings and fly. Just remember that real responsibility comes with every true freedom, and that the magical decisions you make now may last for some time to come.

With that in mind, use this period to cut useless ties and forge new alliances in both the personal and professional realms. Plagued with bad habits or poor health? Now's the time to get both under control. Need a shot of courage, a dose of productivity, or a heaping helping of good old-fashioned energy? Now's the time to get those, too. With the active, building, reconstructing characteristics of Aquarius in the spotlight, almost any effort will meet with success—as long as it centers around you.

This period also brings the festival of Imbolc, the time when we sweep away Winter to make room for Spring. As such, take some time to prepare Brid's bed as a symbolic measure of preparation for the personal growing, greening period that awaits you. Use this period, as well, to ask the blessing of the strengthening Sun on any candles you plan to use throughout the year.

Should the Storm Moon rise during this period, set aside some time for an inner journey. Determine what's important to you, what's not, and what needs to take priority. Then do whatever's necessary to set things in place. If the Wolf Moon rises instead, spend some quality time with those you consider family, including your friends and the Deities. Mend rifts as necessary, strengthen relationships, and enjoy your time together.

Aquarius Sun Sample Invocation

O Great Individualist—Aquarius Sun
Bring forth Your tools so our work can be done
Lend us Your strength and Your dedication
As we clear out the rubble and build new foundations
Teach us of freedom, to ponder and muse
As we reshape ideas into those we can use
As we plan and construct and we build and reform
Aquarius, we welcome Your rays bright and warm

Aquarius Sun Circle Ideas

- Dress in white to welcome the Aquarius Sun.

- Use white and silver candles on the altar, and burn Aquarius incense. (To make your own incense, use a mixture of jasmine, lavender, patchouli, and vetivert.)

- Decorate with Legos, building blocks, and Lincoln Logs. Other ideas might include decorating with bits of abstract art or other creatively expressive art forms.

- Mark the Circle boundary with Legos, with each Quarter being the appropriate color. Cast the Circle with a wooden wand tied with silver and white ribbons.

- Serve hot, spiced orange juice (stir a teaspoon each of powdered cinnamon and clove into the orange juice, then heat and serve), and spice cake for libation.

Aquarius Sun Party Ideas

- Decorate with the colors and items suggested in the Circle Ideas section.

- Because Aquarius energy is all about change and fresh perspective, this is the perfect time for a multi-cultural dinner menu. And this isn't as difficult as you might think. Just pick dishes from other cultures—a salad from one, an entrée from another, and so on—and serve them together. Everyone will get to sample something they've never had before, and the theme of diversity will reign supreme.

- Serve each attendee a Sunshine Cooler. (Please see the Celebratory Drink appendix for recipe.) For non-alcoholic drinks, serve hot, spiced orange juice. Then offer a toast to the Sun by saying something like:

This toast is to You, dear Aquarius Sun
For Your freewheeling thoughts
On how things should be done
For bringing ideas and reshaping our plans
And proving that life is not out of our hands
But that it's in our power to be whom we may
We toast You, Aquarius, upon this fine day

- Provide a box of Legos and have a creative building contest. (No instructions allowed.) Give a prize for the most original and best-planned structure.

- Provide a small pot, some soil, and three beans (pinto or kidney beans work well here) for all attendees, with the instructions to name each bean for a quality they want to bring into their lives. Have them plant the beans with the knowledge that as the beans sprout and grow, so will the characteristics within them.

- Give a simple wooden building block—with the appropriate initial, of course—to each attendee as a party favor.

Sun in Pisces (February 19–March 20)

Thematic Energy: Hooray for the Pisces Sun! At long last, here's a Sun Whose message not only involves contemplation, meditation, and planning, but Who gives us license to kick back, relax, and be still. The key word for the Pisces Sun is "contemplation." And after all that erratic Aquarian energy, we could certainly use some of that! Don't misunderstand, though. There's still work to do. It's just that this Sun allows us to slow down and ponder what we're doing and why, and how it will affect our personal futures. The inner journey is at the forefront, and all we have to do is jump on board.

The Earth is experiencing Her Own inner journey just now, too. With the ice and snow in the melting stages, She yawns and stretches beneath the surface, then looks at Her plans for the busy season ahead. And with that, the initial stages of the growing season take root. The long, spiky leaves of bulbs push through the ground, and wildflowers begin to color the countryside. It's going to be a glorious season, all right, and all because Mother Nature, in Her infinite wisdom, planned properly.

Mundane Energy: The Pisces Sun is a welcome relief because it gives us license to slow down and just be. And no other sign under the Sun allows us that luxury. That doesn't mean there's time to waste, though. This period is reserved for putting mind, body, and spirit back together and aligning them so they can function again as a single, smoothly operating unit. And to make that happen, we have to take some time to tickle the senses.

Start by listening to some music or delving into a good book. Tease your brain a bit by working a crossword puzzle, a jigsaw puzzle, or maybe even playing a video game in which pieces fit together. Visit an art gallery, a museum, or make arrangements to get to that exhibit you've been dying to see. Dance, stretch, or incorporate a low impact workout into your daily routine. Write, draw, and sing. Pull out your favorite divinatory device—card, runes, pendulum, whatever—and brush up on your skills. But above all, meditate. Contemplate where you've been and where you are. Think about where you're going and where you'd like to be. Then put things in place to make sure you get there.

Magical Energy: With the Pisces Sun in the spotlight, inner journeys take precedence, so this is an excellent time for meditation, for forming solid connections with the spiritual realm, and for learning the art of balance between the worlds. Anything that involves psychism, clairvoyance, or divination is a good bet, and efforts that require some sort of illusion or glamoury to meet with success work well now, too. This is also the perfect atmosphere for manifesting inspiration, so if you have problems getting the idea pool to flow free, now's the time to work a little creativity magic. Don't discount this energy for resolving emotional issues, either. There's simply no better Sun than Pisces to get those things taken care of, once and for all.

If the festival of Ostara occurs during this period, use its energy to bring total balance—emotional, mental, and spiritual—into your life, and to fertilize the creative flow. It's also wonderful for workings designed to wake the unconscious and subconscious minds, and put them back into sync with the conscious mind.

If the Chaste Moon rises during this period, use its energy to get back in touch with your Inner Child. Play, laugh, and do some of the things you enjoyed when you were younger. (This might include something like coloring, jumping rope, playing hopscotch, or finger painting.) Whatever you choose will definitely please your Inner Child, and there's nothing better to increase the creative flow of your magic.

Should the Seed Moon rise instead, spend some time thinking about how your magic germinates. Go over spells and make any necessary changes. Write new rituals. Give some thought to any magic you intend to perform in the coming months. It's the best time of all to prepare your spiritual garden for a healthy crop of magical manifestation.

Pisces Sun Sample Invocation

Come to us, Pisces—Compassionate Sun

Teach us to journey as we've never done

Take us at once to the innermost core

And help us to heal wounds forgotten and sore

Bring emotional issues to the forefront as well

So we may get past them; with Your light dispel

Our fears and whatever else clouds up our minds

We welcome You, Pisces—in Your light we shine

Pisces Sun Circle Ideas

- Dress in shades of blue and green to welcome the Pisces Sun.

- Use blue and green candles on the altar, and burn Pisces incense. (To make your own incense, use a mixture of orris root, vanilla, and patchouli.)

- Decorate the altar with flowers of the season or a pot of flowering bulbs. Ribbon-tied bunches of candles are appropriate, as well, to symbolize the return of warmth to the Earth.

- Line the Circle boundary with tarot cards, runes, or other divinatory tools, and cast the Circle with a seashell or seashell-tipped wand.

- Serve peppermint schnapps, or peppermint tea, and chocolate-covered mint cookies for libation.

Pisces Sun Party Ideas

- Decorate with the colors and items suggested in the Circle Ideas section.

- Since Pisces puts us in a kick-back-and-ponder sort of mood, comfort foods are in order; in fact, you might want to make this a dessert-only party. Should you decide to go this route, just supply the champagne (the inexpensive sort is fine) and ginger ale, and ask each guest to bring his or her favorite after-meal dish. And if you think snacks are necessary before the dessert-fest begins, serve goldfish crackers with cheese or salmon dip.

- Serve each attendee a Mimosa. (Please see the Celebratory Drink appendix for recipe.) For non-alcoholic drinks, serve orange juice mixed half and half with ginger ale. Then offer a toast to the Sun by saying something like:

  O Pisces—Great Sun Who shines from within
  Who heals all old wounds with the flick of a fin
  Who takes us on journeys that go to the core
  And clears out emotional messes and more
  Who tickles our psyche with His divine might
  Here's to You, Pisces—we drink to Your light

- Because this is the time to slow down and re-group, you might make this party a magical movie-fest. Just pick out three or four movies with a magical theme— *Lord of the Rings, Excalibur, The Mists of Avalon,* or even the *Harry Potter* movies are good ideas—and let the DVD player do the rest.

- Go on a group outing to a museum of history or tour a home of historical value in your area. Pay special attention to the paths of those involved, and the steps they took to fulfill their goals. Contemplate that knowledge, and apply it toward your inner journey and toward any plans for your future.

- Small notebooks and brightly-colored pencils with fish-shaped erasers make excellent party favors.

Endnote

1. There are many versions of the Charge. Mine is inserted here for your convenience, but feel free to use whatever version you like.

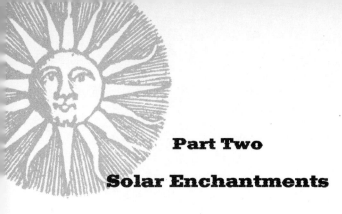

Part Two

Solar Enchantments

Mine is the success, for I am the Sun
I manifest efforts as magic is spun
With Me, there's no problem, no fuss, and no wait
Results are immediate and culminate
In total victory for the petitioner
For I'm the best friend of every practitioner
Whether energy, health, or matters of heart
Cash flow, separation, or gaining new starts
Is what you visualize in your mind's eye
I bring it quickly and never deny
That which you wish or that of which you dream
No matter how small or how large or extreme
For I am the All: Father, Lover, and Child
The Brother, the Sage, and the Warrior, so wild
I am the Grandfather of dwindling time
I am the Sun—I am Magic sublime

—Dorothy Morrison

Here it is: the spell section you've been waiting for! In fact, it's a safe bet that many of you turned directly to this page without even looking at the rest of the book. And while it's certainly not the most effective way to use the information here—and you'll be missing out on a lot if you don't read the rest of this book first—that's okay. It's just the human factor at work.

Because of this, though, there are a few things that bear mention before delving into this section. And such is the reason for this note.

For starters, you'll notice that a good many of the spells outlined here call for either working outdoors beneath the Sun, or from a window facing in a particular direction. Furthermore, some spells require that the rays of the Sun shine directly on an object to absorb His energy. And for many reasons—cloud cover, rain, snow, or maybe even the simple lack of a window that faces in the proper direction—meeting these requirements isn't always possible. Not to worry, though. It doesn't mean that you can't perform these spells, that you have to wait until the proper weather conditions avail themselves, or that you have to cut a hole in your wall.

So, what do you do? How do you handle these problems? More to the point, how can you expect to perform successful magic if there's no way to meet the proper conditions?

Simply put, you learn to think outside the box.

Regardless of the weather conditions, just remember that the Sun is still there in the sky. It doesn't matter whether or not you can see Him. He still rises in the morning and sinks below the horizon in the evening. And as such, His energies are always present during the day. It's just a matter of looking at things logically instead of at what seems apparent.

But what about the window thing? How can that be resolved?

Not to worry there, either. While having the proper window is definitely an advantage, this problem can be handled in several ways. If you're performing the effort on a sunny day, for example, you can simply take the object in question outdoors to absorb the proper energy. You can also place the item in a sunny spot in your home. And if neither of those options are viable? Try a bit of creative visualization. Just fashion a window in your mind's eye, and see the light streaming into the item and saturating it with the necessary energy. It's as simple as that.

One other thing: Remember that you are the practitioner, and as such, *you* make the magic happen. It comes from your ability to move and direct the energy at hand. And all the proper tools or materials—or in this case, appropriate weather conditions—in the world aren't going to change that. It's your desire that sets the magic in motion, your focus that brings it to manifestation, and once you've reconciled yourself to that, there's no reason in the world that your efforts should ever meet with anything other than success.

5

Dawn: Infant/Young Child Sun Efforts

The general period for working the spells in this section is between Sunrise and approximately 9:00 a.m. Unless otherwise specified, those spells that utilize the energy of the Infant Sun are best performed at Sunrise, while those incorporating the energy of the Young Child Sun can enjoy success when performed right up until 9:00 a.m. Efforts that invoke both phases, however, may be performed at any time during the period.

Acceptance

Sun Tea Spell for Acceptance and Tolerance

Materials

½ teaspoon tarragon

1 paper coffee filter

3 family-size tea bags

1 quart cold water

Quart jar with screw-on lid

Twine or string

Sprinkle the tarragon in the center of the coffee filter, then gather the edges to form a bag, and secure well with string. Toss the tea bags and tarragon bag in the jar, fill it with cold water, screw on the lid, and take it outdoors. Holding the jar up to the Sun, ask His help by saying something like:

> *O Growing Child—Our Sun and Star—*
>
> *Cast Your rays both near and far*
>
> *Upon this tea and bless it well*
>
> *So that its properties expel*
>
> *Worn-out notions and perceptions*
>
> *Old ideas and misconceptions*
>
> *And as You brew it, please imbue*
>
> *It with an accepting, tolerant view*
>
> *Of those things I find so difficult*
>
> *So its ingestion shall result*
>
> *In a freedom that I've never known*
>
> *From expectations that I've sown*
>
> *In others' gardens as they tread*
>
> *Their personal paths; and please, too, shed*
>
> *Your light upon me—guide my way—*
>
> *As I work through this today*
>
> *O Young Child Sun, now hear my plea*
>
> *And do just what I ask of Thee*

Place the jar in a sunny spot and leave it there to brew until Sunset.

Remove the bags and dilute if necessary. Sweeten as desired, and drink.

Beauty
Avocado Facial Mask Spell

Materials

1 avocado

Blender, food processor, or hand mixer

Take the avocado outdoors and face east. (If this isn't possible, take it to an eastern window in your home.) Then, holding it up to the Sun, ask His assistance by saying something like:

O Infant Sun, Who streaks the sky

With Your beauty, low and high

And with Your radiance, so new

I now implore You to imbue

This fruit with all Your glowing splendor

And charge its pulp so that it renders

Beautiful s/he who applies

It to the face—and brings demise

To every flaw and imperfection—

And brings a radiant complexion

O Infant Sun, I conjure You

Charge this fruit with beauty, true

Leave the avocado in the east for several hours—two or three should do the trick—then peel and deseed. Process the pulp on high for a few minutes until smooth. Then apply the paste to clean skin and leave it on for fifteen minutes. During the waiting period, chant something like:

> *Mine is beauty—splendor's mine*
> *Like the Rising Sun, I shine*

Rinse well with warm water, and pat dry.

Beginnings

Orange Juice Spell for a Fresh Start

Materials

Small glass of orange juice

Take the juice outside at daybreak and, facing east, offer it to the Infant Sun by saying something like:

> *O Infant born into the sky*
> *I offer this to You on high*
> *And offer thanks for Your arrival*
> *And for the role You play in our survival*

Turning clockwise, pour the juice on the ground in a circle around you. Then ask the Sun for a fresh start by saying something like:

> *O Infant Sun, I call to You*
> *Who starts each day with life anew*

Whose birth brings warmth and gives us joy

Whose light the darkness does destroy

Who separates the night from day

Who guides us with His gentle rays

Who gives us hope and makes us smile

Who makes each step we take worthwhile

Who inspires and cultivates

Fresh ideas and captivates

All who feel His golden light

I ask You, Infant Sun, so bright

To bring to me a new beginning

That puts me on the path to winning

What I desire most in my life—

Free of needless stress and strife—

Oh, bring to me a fresh new start

And I ask You, too, impart

Your courage as I tread anew

The path that I now ask of You

Bring this at once now, Infant Sun

As I will, so be it done

Kiss your hand to the Sun and step over the juice circle.
Go indoors and know that a brand new beginning is on
its way.

Change
Fern Spell

Materials

1 small fern of any variety

1 6-inch pot with drainage holes

1 plastic saucer to fit pot

Potting soil

Gather your materials and take them outdoors an hour or two after daybreak. Repot the fern, place the saucer beneath it, and fill the saucer with water. As the plant soaks up the water, visualize the desired change taking place precisely as you wish. Then ask the Young Child Sun and the spirit of the fern to effect the desired change by saying something like:

Young Child Sun of smiling eyes

And Soul of Fern, You now comprise

A powerful team of transformation

To bring about the alteration

I desire with Your entwined

Powers, just as I've designed

Bring it smoothly—make it gentle—

Without snag or supplemental

Aggravation. And as you grow

Beneath this Sun of warmest glow

Little fern, this change ensues

Accomplishing what it should do

Until the time it manifests
And even then, You cannot rest
For new fronds keep this change effective
I conjure You both to this directive

Keep the fern outdoors or in a sunny window, and water it from the saucer once each week.

To Ease Transition

Materials
9 fertilizer sticks
1 4-inch square of yellow fabric
   or a yellow handkerchief

Gather the fertilizer sticks and fabric and go out to locate a cypress tree. (If cypress isn't indigenous to your area, not to worry. A fir tree of any type will do in a pinch.) Then beseech the tree to ease your current transition by saying something like:

O tree of needles ever green
Who endures change that's seldom seen
Ease the changes in my life
Bring them, please, without the strife
That often accompanies real transition
Make them not an imposition
But rather, a tool with which to work
An implement of many perks

Gather a few needles from the ground. (If there aren't any needles on the ground, ask the tree for a few, and wait for its answer. It's very unlikely that the tree will refuse you, but if it does, go on to another tree.) Place the needles in the cloth or handkerchief, tie the ends tightly to secure them, and put the parcel at the base of the tree.

Holding the fertilizer sticks in your hands and offering them to the tree, say something like:

And for lending Your assistance, Tree

I bring this gift to offer Thee

To aid Your growth, to aid Your life

To ease whatever stress and strife

Comes to You from helping me

I give these to You thankfully

Visualizing the tree remaining healthy for many years to come, push the first stick into the ground directly in front of you, but close to the base of the tree. Then, working in a clockwise manner and still visualizing the good health of the tree, place the remaining sticks evenly around the base as well.

Pick up the parcel, thank the tree for its gift, and ask its blessing, saying something like:

I thank You for Your aid this day

And as I go about my way

I ask your blessing on the morsel

Of Yourself within this parcel
Grant that it brings Your strength to me
As I will, so mote it be

Wait a few moments, then leave. Carry the parcel with you until the transition is complete.

Creativity
Crayon Charm Spell

Materials
1 purple candle
1 yellow crayon
1 red crayon
1 blue crayon
1 green crayon
1 24-inch length of purple ribbon

Begin this spell within two hours of Sunrise by placing the candle in front of you and lighting the wick, saying something like:

I call to You, O Young Child Sun
With this flame, the spell's begun
Bring to light creative flow
I conjure You to make it so

Place the yellow crayon on the eastern side of the candle, and say something like:

With yellow now, I call You, Air
Winds of change and breezes fair
Bring fresh ideas at once to me
As I will, so mote it be

Place the red crayon on the southern side of the candle, and say something like:

By red, I call the flames of Fire
Who bring forth passion and desire
Kindle creativity
As I will, so mote it be

Place the blue crayon on the western side of the candle, and say something like:

And Water, I now call with blue
Babbling brooks and morning dew
Let idea pools now flow free
As I will, so mote it be

Place the green crayon on the northern side of the candle, and say something like:

By green, I call upon Earth's power
Of forests, fields, and mountain towers
Fertilize creativity
As I will, so mote it be

Then turn your palms upward and beseech the Elements and the Young Child Sun by saying something like:

Elements and Young Child Sun
I conjure You to work as One
Bring Your gifts at once to me
And spark my creativity

After the candle has burned for at least an hour, collect the crayons in a clockwise manner, beginning with the yellow and ending with the green. Place the crayon bundle in the center of the ribbon, wrap the ends of the ribbon around the bundle three times, and tie. Repeat the wrap and tie the ends into a bow. Place the bundle in front of the candle and leave it there until the wick burns out.

Hang the crayon charm over your work area.

Employment
New Job Resume Spell

Materials
Copies of your resume

Place the copies of your resume where they can catch the first rays of morning Sun, and hold your hands over them, saying something like:

Infant Sun, so fresh and new
I implore You to imbue
These resumes with true success
And with Your light, I ask You bless

Them, too, with power as You grow
So that they shine from every stack—
And cannot fall between the cracks—
Of applications and resumes
Let mine find an entryway
Into the hands that offer me
The perfect job; so mote it be

Lick your forefinger and use it to mark the back of each page with an equal-armed cross surrounded by a clockwise circle. Mail or deliver the resumes, and know that the perfect job is on its way.

Fresh Perspective
Prayer to the Infant Sun for Fresh Perspective

O Infant Sun, illuminate
The views I haven't seen to date
I ask You, too, to cast Your light
On angles hidden from my sight
Grant me, too, an open mind
So that new avenues I find
Help me to see all things anew
Do now what I ask of You

Friendship
Wildflower Spell to Gain New Friends

Materials
1 package wildflower seeds

Take the package of seeds outdoors two to three hours after Sunrise. Facing the Sun and holding your arms out as if to embrace Him, state your request by saying something like:

> *I implore You, Young Child Sun,*
> *To extend my circle of friends and fun*
> *From east and west and south and north*
> *Bring all kindred spirits forth*
> *Bring those with whom I can share*
> *Love and laughter, and who care*
> *About the same things that I do*
> *Let a common thread run through*
> *Our interests; give us time to know*
> *Each other so that friendship grows*

Rip open the package of seeds and toss them in a clockwise circle around you, saying something like:

> *And as these seeds take root and sprout*
> *Weave a system of support throughout*
> *The friendships that You've brought to me*
> *As I will, so mote it be*

Growth
Spell for Personal Growth

Materials
1 green candle
1 yellow candle
1 white candle

Begin this spell on Sunday sometime between Sunrise and three hours after by placing the green candle in front of you, and the yellow and white candles on its left and right, respectively. Light the green candle, then the yellow and white, and visualize yourself growing and blossoming into what you were born to be. Then ask the Young Sun's assistance by saying something like:

Young Sun, as You grow today

In strength and light and other ways

Bring Your growth as well to me

Mentally and spiritually

Cast light, too, on my emotions

So I may check all worn-out notions

And cast all far away from me

That hinder what my growth should be

Push me forth into progression

Step by step in smooth succession

And I ask, too, O Young Child Sun

To make these growing lessons fun

So I blossom easily

As I will, so mote it be

Reflect on your personal growth for fifteen minutes, then snuff out the candles. Repeat the spell each day through the following Sunday. On the last day, let the candles extinguish themselves.

Health

Sick Room Smudge

Materials

1 tablespoon dried mistletoe

1 tablespoon dried eucalyptus

1 tablespoon dried lavender

2 tablespoons dried cedar needles or bark

Charcoal block

Censer or fireproof dish

Blender or food processor

Toss the mistletoe, eucalyptus, lavender, and cedar into the blender or food processor, and process on high for about thirty seconds. Then, holding your hands over the mixture, charge it by saying something like:

Herbs combined, I conjure You

To eradicate germs and to pursue

All viruses and other stuff

That makes us sick—or just feel rough—

To eliminate bacteria

Heed now this criteria

So as you burn, your smoke will kill

Everything that causes ill

A healing smudge, you now shall be

As I will, so mote it be

Burn the mixture a tablespoon at a time on a charcoal block, and use it to smudge a sick room. (It can also be used as a preventative measure to cleanse the entire home.) Store any leftover smudge in a zippered bag.

Heartbreak

Charm to Dispel Heartbreak

Materials

1 yellow candle

2 tablespoons thyme, dried

1 4-inch square of yellow fabric
    or a yellow handkerchief

1 small piece of blue sunstone

Vegetable oil

Anoint the candle in vegetable oil and roll it in one tablespoon of thyme. Light the candle and place the yellow fabric in front of it. Then hold the sunstone to your third eye while willing the stone to absorb all heartbreak. Place the stone on top of the fabric, saying something like:

Bluest stone with glittered face

Absorb the hurt within this space

I call my heart—please take it all

Away from me—now heed my call

Sprinkle the remaining thyme on top of the stone, and say something like:

Herb of joy, now fill the space

Left by the stone of glittered face

Fill my heart with warmth and care

So only joy is present there

Tie the ends of the fabric to secure the parcel, and leave it in front of the candle. Place your hands over the parcel and say something like:

I conjure You, both herb and stone

To work together to dethrone

The heartache that's been plaguing me

As I will, so mote it be

Leave the parcel in front of the candle until the wick extinguishes itself, then carry the parcel over your heart for seven days. On the eighth day, bury the parcel at a crossroads (or as close as you can get to one).

Hope

Prayer to the Young Sun for Hope

O Youngest Sun, grant me the scope

Of Your childlike, joyous hope

Put depression on the run

And illuminate the good to come

So that I see it easily

And of pessimism, I am free

Be my beacon and the light

That exudes hope, both warm and bright;

And bring that light at once to me

As I will, so mote it be

Joy

Prism Spell

Materials

1 prism for each window in the home

Either take the prisms outside just before Sunrise, or place them in a spot where they will catch the first rays of the morning Sun. As the Sun begins to rise, place your hands over them and ask the Infant Sun to charge them by saying something like:

Infant Sun, so new and bright

Infuse these prisms with Your light

Smile on them with warmth and love

And lend Your laughter from above

Lend, too, Your mirth and happiness

As well as childlike joy and bliss

So none who see them or who feel

Their power can resist the real

Delight with which they are imbued

Or the wondrous awe that they exude

O Infant Sun, now hear my plea

And charge these prisms with Your glee

Leave the prisms in the sunlight for three hours, and then hang one in each window of your home.

Love

Apple Spell for True Love

Materials

1 apple

1 6-inch square of red fabric or a red handkerchief

Slice the apple crosswise to reveal the perfect seeded star inside. Eat half the apple while visualizing the perfect mate entering your life. Then take the fabric and the other half of the apple outdoors—or to a place where you can see the Sun—and hold it up in offering, saying something like:

By Sun and Fruit and Perfect Star

Search the land both near and far

To find the perfect love for me
As I will, so mote it be

Starting by removing the seed that forms the lower left-hand arm of the star and placing it in the fabric, say something like:

By Newborn Sun that grows above

Working in a clockwise manner, pluck the next seed from the apple and place it in the fabric, saying:

By Adolescent's first real love

Pluck the next seed and place it in the fabric, saying:

By Father's warmth that fills the heart

Pluck the next seed and place it in the fabric, saying:

By Sage's truth and Warrior's dart

Pluck the last seed and place it in the fabric, saying:

By Sacrificial Sun's bequest

Tie the ends of the fabric together to secure the seeds, then hold the parcel up to the Sun, saying something like:

I conjure You—heed my request—
Work together, work as One
All phases of the Brilliant Sun
To bring the perfect mate to me
As I will, so mote it be

Leave the apple outside for the animals, and carry the parcel with you until your perfect love arrives.

Physical Energy
Quartz Crystal Re-Energizing Charm

Materials
1 clear quartz crystal

Place the stone where it can catch the first rays of Sunrise, then place your hands over it and enchant it by saying something like:

> *Rays of Sun, now add Your power*
> *To this stone with every hour*
> *'Til it's saturated with Your light*
> *Your energy, and all Your might*

Leave the stone there until noon, then hold it in both hands and see yourself easily moving through the day without being tired. Enchant the stone further by saying something like:

> *Clearest energizing stone*
> *I ask your powers to me loan*
> *When energy begins to sway*
> *Revitalize me through the day*
> *Re-energize as necessary*
> *Muscle, bone, flesh, and capillary*
> *So I may easily adjust*

To handle all the things I must

Exude at once, your energy

As I will, so mote it be

Carry the stone with you.

Psychic Ability

Psychic Awakening/Blockage Removal Tea

Materials

2 tablespoons mugwort, dried

1 coffee filter

1 quart cold water

Quart jar with screw-on lid

String

Place the mugwort in the coffee filter, secure with string, and toss into the jar. Add the water, secure the lid, and take the jar outdoors. Offer it to the Sun by saying something like:

O Youngest Sun of golden rays

Lend to this tea Your fiery blaze

To waken my abilities

Toward psychic possibilities

Destroy all psychic stumbling blocks

And open all my psychic locks

So that there are no blockages

To impede the messages

That come to me through day and night

I ask, too, that You shed Your light

Upon unclear communications

To aid in my determinations

Of their meanings; I ask, too,

That as You bless and charge this brew

You keep me in Your sight as well

And bless me as You bless this spell

Place the jar in a sunny spot and leave it there until Sunset, allowing the mixture to brew.

Remove the bag, dilute if necessary, and sweeten as desired. Drink one cup before embarking on psychic activities or exercises.

Tools

General Consecration

Materials

Tool to be consecrated

Hold the tool up to the Sun in offering, and say something like:

I consecrate this tool to You

O Sun, and ask that You imbue

It with the ever-growing, bright

Splendor of Your brilliant light,

Your strength, and with Your energy,

With every capability

That You hold and that You are

O perfect, shining, blazing Star
I consecrate this tool to You
Infuse it well that it may do
The job for which it was intended—
A job no less than truly splendid—
And reflect Your power, once set free
As I will, so mote it be

Leave the tool in the sunlight until Sunset, then store it in the same fashion as your other magical tools.

Trust
Spell to Dispel Distrust

Materials
1 pink or peach candle
1 tablespoon yarrow, dried
1 small piece of amethyst
Vegetable oil

Anoint the candle with vegetable oil, roll it in the yarrow, and light the wick. Hold the stone in your hands and visualize yourself trusting again without being harmed. Then place the stone in front of the candle and ask the assistance of the Young Child Sun by saying something like:

By wax, stone, herb, and Sun of gold
I melt away distrust's stronghold

I beseech You, Sun, expose my heart

And burn away the very part

That holds my trust within its walls

The part that can resist the calls

Of friendship and sincerity

The part that begs to be set free

But cowers from the damage done

In the past by more than one

So Childlike Sun, Your strength, please lend—

Your courage, too—and bring an end

To any fears that dwell inside

And allow Your golden light to guide

My heart in trust and love once more

I beg You Sun—fling forth the door

Let the wick extinguish itself, then carry the stone with you.

Weather

Spell for Fair Weather

Materials

1 small package unsalted sunflower seeds

Go outdoors at dawn, and empty the seeds into your hands. Toss a few seeds to the east and say:

Air, come hither

Toss a few seeds to the south and say:

> *Fire, come, too*

Toss a few seeds to the west and north, and say:

> *Water and Earth, I call to You*

Then, working in a clockwise motion, scatter the remaining seeds around you in a circle a few at a time, while saying something like:

> *Work together—work as One—*
> *And bring to me the shining Sun*
> *Keep His light both strong and bright*
> *Until the dusk is claimed by night*
> *Bring to me a warm, fair day*
> *I conjure You; do as I say*

Wishes
Wishing Rune Spell

Materials

1 teaspoon mistletoe, fresh (readily available
    year-round at florist shops)
¼ cup vegetable oil
1 orange candle
Pen and paper
Food processor or blender
Small bottle with tight-fitting lid

Begin by pureeing the mistletoe and oil in a food processor or blender (be sure to sterilize the device thoroughly after use, as ingestion of mistletoe is hazardous to good health). Then pour the mixture into the bottle. Inscribe the candle with the wishing rune shown in figure 14, and write your wish in the center of the circle. Draw the same rune on the paper, and write your wish in the center of the circle there, as well. Anoint the candle with a few drops of the mistletoe oil, and light it, while visualizing your wish manifesting precisely as you desire.

Place the paper in front of the candle and, starting at the center of the rune and using a few drops of the oil, anoint the rune by moving your fingers up to the upper right-hand corner. Repeat the process from the center to the lower right-hand corner, from the center to the lower left-hand corner, and from the center to the upper left-hand corner. Say something like:

I give you life and feed you, Rune
With my wish, you're now attuned
Bring me what I ask of thee
As I will, so mote it be

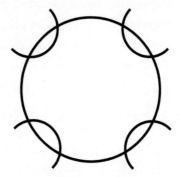

Figure 14: Wishing Rune

Leave the paper in front of the candle until the candle wick burns out, then keep the paper in a safe place where you'll see it every day. Anoint the rune with the oil weekly to feed it. When your wish comes true, burn the paper and scatter the ashes on the winds.

6

Morning: Adolescent Brother/Lover Sun Efforts

The general period for working the spells in this section is between 9:00 a.m. and 11:00 a.m. Unless otherwise specified, those spells that utilize the energy of the Adolescent Brother Sun tend to be most successful when performed during the first hour of this time frame, while those spells pertaining to the Lover Sun enjoy more success when performed during the latter. Efforts that invoke both phases, however, may be performed at any time during the period.

Communication
Get in Touch Spell

Materials
Paper
Pen
Vanilla oil (vanilla extract will work in a pinch)
Adhesive tape

Start by writing your name on the paper, and drawing an ear next to it. (Not to worry. The Universe doesn't care if you're an artist. It only matters that you know what the drawing represents.) Below that, write the name of the person who should contact you, and beside it, draw a pair of lips. Moisten your fingers with a few drops of the oil and, beginning at the center of the paper, move your fingers in a diagonal line to the upper right-hand corner. Starting at the center again, repeat the motion to lower right-hand corner, the lower left-hand corner, and the upper left-hand corner. As you anoint the paper, say something like:

> *By ears and lips, by pen and oil*
> *The urge to get in touch now boils*
> *It churns until you cannot rest*
> *It burns until you meet this quest*
> *Not stopping 'til you contact me*
> *As I will, so mote it be*

The next step depends on the type of contact information the person in question is likely to have for you. If it's an e-mail address, tape the paper to your computer. If it's a phone number, fix it to the bottom of your phone. A snail address would require attaching it to the inside of your mailbox. You get the idea. Just tape the paper in the most appropriate place, and know that it will do the job.

Courage
Hematite Charm

Materials

1 small piece of hematite

Start by holding the stone in your hands and feeling its calming energy wash over you. Take several deep breaths and allow the stone to help you to ground and center, then enchant the stone by saying something like:

Iron ore stone of hematite

Stone of ancient wars and fights

Stone of arrow heads and spears

And weaponry, cast out my fears

Be a charm of bravery

As I will, so mote it be

Then hold the stone up to the Sun and request His assistance by saying something like:

Courageous Adolescent Sun

Bravest God of Any One

Who's bulletproof and ten feet tall

Bless this stone and hear this call

Lend Your courage to my heart

Banish fear from every part

Of my spirit and my soul

Guide me well and take control

Of my valor and my nerve

Help me forge ahead to serve

The causes that are dear to me

As I will, so mote it be

Carry the stone with you, and rub it whenever courage is an issue.

Gardening
Healthy Garden Spell

Materials
4 small pieces of moss agate

Go to the center of your garden or flower bed and, holding the stones up to your third eye, visualize your garden being green and producing an abundance of fruit, vegetables, and/or flowers. Then toss the stones one by one toward the four corners of the plot, saying with each one:

O Active, Fertile Lover Sun

I call upon You, Virile One

To fertilize this garden well

And activate the stones that fell

So that together You'll produce

A healthy garden so profuse

That none has ever seen its kind

By these words, You are assigned

To do these things I ask of Thee

As I will, so mote it be

Bury the stones where they lay, and tend the garden well.

Harmony

Incense Smudging Spell

Materials

Nag Champa incense

Light the incense and visualize its smoke choking out everything that keeps your home from enjoying a pleasant atmosphere. Then use it to thoroughly smudge each room, while saying something like:

By fire of incense and its smoke

I call You, Sun, and now evoke

Your unifying properties

And call upon your expertise

In light and laughter, and in peace

To cause all conflict here to cease

Remove all tension from this place

Along with stress that's interlaced

Through paint and furniture and wall

With your strength, relieve it all

Leaving only harmony

So all those in this space agree

On pleasant terms and peaceful ways
Beginning on this very day
I call on You, O Blazing One
As I will, so be it done

Inspiration
Bird Feeder Spell

Materials
Bird feeder
Wild birdseed

Fill the feeder with seed, and visualize a variety of birds flocking there to eat. See the diverse colors of their plumage, the differences in their attitudes, and the variances in how they interact with each other. Once the images are firmly fixed in your mind's eye, "inspire" the birds to come. That's right. Will them to the feeder. Then ask them to return the favor by saying something like:

Creatures of the Air and Sky
I offer you this food supply
To eat at will, for it is yours
But in your coming, you assure
That you will bring a gift along:
Inspiration, free and strong
On your wings and feathers bright
Loosing it so it shall light
Within my mind and heart and soul

To assist me with my goals
And in return, I promise to
Keep this feeder full for you

Fill the feeder every day, and know that inspiration is forthcoming.

Imagination
Quick Chant for Imagination

O Brightest Adolescent Sun
Bring ideas now on the run
Set my imagination free
And boost my creativity
Bring vision now to leaf and bud
And fertilize that which was mud
Changing it to richest loam
Where thoughts can root and freely roam
And sprout with new simplicity
As I will, so mote it be

Liberation
Quick Liberation Chant

See the Sun burning away all the obstacles in your way, and everything that keeps you from getting ahead. Say something like:

O Primal, Vital growing Sun

Direct Your flames to get this done:

Burn away all the restrictions

That distance me from my convictions

Set the obstacles on fire

That keep me from my heart's desire

Destroy as well what's in the way

Of reaching for my goals today

Flaming Sun, I ask of Thee

Bring true freedom now to me

Obstacles should begin to dissipate in twenty-four hours or less.

Love
Perfect Mate Spell

Materials
1 red candle
1 pink candle
Red pen
Paper
Cigarette lighter
Fireproof dish

Using the red pen, make a list of all the qualities you desire in a perfect mate. Be brutally honest. (Take your time with this, and know that you won't be able to do this in one sitting.) When the list is complete, use the lighter to melt a bit of the wax down the length of one candle, then press the other candle to it firmly to join them together as one. Light the candles and place the list in front of them.

Watch the flames burn for a few moments, then visualize the perfect mate coming to you. (It's important to refrain from putting a face on this person, so you may wish to view him or her from the rear.) See yourselves as best friends. See yourselves in the romance of the century. See yourselves in the heat of hot, wild, passionate sex. Finally, see yourselves growing old together and enjoying each other's company. Place your hands over the list and say something like:

Red and pink and dancing fire

Bring to me what I desire

Precisely what I've written here

And what's envisioned crystal clear

In my mind's eye; it's what I ask

So hearken quickly to this task

Bring perfect love at once to me

As I will, so mote it be

Leave the list in front of the candle until the candle wick burns out. Then take the list outdoors and place it in a fireproof dish. Set the list on fire, and as it burns to ashes, say something like:

As this list now burns to cinder

Lover Sun, with heart so tender,

Illuminate the world so wide

With brightest rays so none can hide

And find for me the perfect mate

Direct his/her path; alleviate

Potential problems in our way—

Like not connecting in the fray

Of busy lives with much to do—

O Lover Sun, I ask You, too,

To bring him/her quickly to my arms

And spark as quickly all the charms

Of real romance and truest love

With Your golden flames above

Bring my love at once to me

As I will, so mote it be

When the ashes are cool, scatter them in a clockwise circle and leave, knowing that the Lover Sun will handle the task at hand.

Lust

Crystal Obelisk Charm

Materials

1 clear quartz crystal obelisk

1 small red lead crystal bowl or red glass bowl

1 red candle

1 teaspoon cloves

1 teaspoon allspice
1 teaspoon ginger
Red rose petals, dried
Cinnamon oil

Take the materials to the bedroom, and begin by placing the obelisk in the center of the bowl. Think about how the two objects symbolize the masculine and feminine, and about what you wish to accomplish. Then cup your hands around the objects and say something like:

Phallic symbol cut from quartz
And bowl, you are now counterparts
Within this spell—this call to lust—
To you, this duty I entrust
As you meet now, start the ache
That only lust for sex can make
That yearning throb and hot desire
Light and kindle passion's fire

Light the candle and place it in back of the objects while visualizing the fires of lust being kindled. Fill the bowl with rose petals and sprinkle the herbs on top of and around the obelisk. Add a few drops of cinnamon oil, then say something like:

Spice and petals, wax and oil
Bring this craving to a boil
But let it simmer first and well—
Saturating every cell

Of those intended, through and through—
Then bring hot sex; I conjure you!

Let the candle wick burn out, then place the lust charm on the dresser or bedside table.

Opportunity
Quick Midmorning Chant for Opportunity

I've never known this chant to fail when it comes to opening a channel of prospects or just bringing a welcome break to a rut-filled life.

Midmorning Sun, fling forth the door
Clear Cosmic halls and corridors
So opportunities flow free
And with Your light, guide them to me

Passion
Prayer to Overcome the Doldrums

Sun of gold and blazing fire
I ask that You ignite desire
And spark again true passion's flame
So that once again, I claim
Its benefits in work and play
And feel its rush in every day
Like fresh excitement and its thrill
The gusto that just soars at will

The enthusiasm that it knows

And exhilarating way it flows

Through every fiber that it reaches

And the way that it beseeches

Me to do my very best

Bring passion now to manifest

I ask You, Sun, to set it free

And bring it now—at once, to me

Personal Empowerment
Seed Spell

Materials

1 purple candle

1 package flower seeds (good choices
   are sweet peas, sunflowers, or dahlias,
   as they're easy to grow)

Flower pot and soil (optional)

Light the candle and set the seed package in front of it.
See yourself as empowered, being able to live any life
you choose, and becoming whomever you wish. Then
raise your hands, palms up, and implore the Sun to
help you in the quest by saying something like:

Ten feet tall and bulletproof

Though independent, not aloof

These qualities describe You, Sun

O Adolescent Shining One

You are empowered by Your flame

And by a courage none can tame

O Sun, instill these things in me

And guide me so that I can free

The seeds of my own personal power

Bring them bud and leaf and shower

Them with all they need to grow

As I will, Sun, make it so

Leave the package in front of the candle until the wick burns out, then plant the seeds and water them well. (If you need to plant them indoors, use the flower pot.) Remember to tend the seeds, for as they grow, so will your personal power.

Productivity
To-Do List Spell

Materials
1 purple candle
1 tablespoon allspice
Vegetable oil
Your to-do list

Anoint the candle with vegetable oil, then roll it in the allspice. Place your to-do list in front of the candle and light the wick. Visualize everything on the list as completed and marked off. Then ask the Adolescent Sun to help you get everything done by saying something like:

Sun of growing energy
Lend Your productivity
Lend Your power—lend Your strength
Work with me and stay at length
Help me now to get through this
Ever-growing to-do list
And as this flame melts through the wax
Push Your powers to the max
To mark off things and get them done
Assist me, Adolescent Sun
In this quest for true efficiency
As I will, so mote it be

Pick up the to-do list and work on only one thing at a time. Let the candle burn while you work, and scratch off tasks on your list as you complete them. Allow the wick to extinguish itself.

Prosperity
Money-Draw Charm

Materials
1 green candle
1 penny
1 nickel
1 dime
1 quarter
1 small magnet

    9 fish hooks

    5 teaspoons basil, dried

    5 teaspoons cinnamon, dried

    5 teaspoons orange peel, dried

    Green bottle with a cork (available at
       arts and crafts stores)

Place all of the materials in front of the candle and light the wick. Put the coins in the bottle one at a time, while saying something like:

Penny, nickel, quarter, dime

Multiply in double time

Drop the magnet in and say:

Magnet, draw the cash to me

Drop the hooks in one at a time and say:

Hooks, grab it tight as it can be

Sprinkle the spices over the top and say:

Spices, do your thing as well

To make this money grow and swell

Then offer the bottle to the Sun and say:

And Sun, shine brightly on this stash

To keep the flow of ready cash

Coming toward me every day

By my command, do as I say

Using the candle, drop a bit of melted wax on the edges of the cork, and push the cork firmly into the bottle to seal it. Say something like:

By magnet and hook, by spice and coin

The fibers of this spell now join

By color of money, by light of Sun

The magic of this spell is spun

By melted wax, this spell is sealed

Cash charm you are—cash you shall yield

Leave the bottle in front of the candle until the wick extinguishes itself, then place the bottle in a sunny spot in your home—a windowsill works well—where the golden rays of the Sun will shine on it each day.

Romance

Spell to Kindle Romance

Materials

1 pink rose bud, fresh

1 pink candle

Bud vase filled with water

Place the rose bud in the vase and set it in front of the candle. As you light the wick, say something like:

Pink wax and dancing flame, so free

Bring romance at once to me

Hold your hands around the vase and allow yourself to feel and enjoy its energy. Then say something like:

Romantic symbol, pinkest rose

Bring to me what I want most

Romantic love and all its pleasure

As I will, provide this treasure

Then, holding the vase aloft in offering to the Sun, say something like:

Fires of Adolescent Sun

And that of Lover, too, now come

With golden rays, enchant this flower

And lend to it Your blazing power

So it brings the playful fun

Of fresh romance that's just begun

All its warmth and all its joy

Ignite the sparks that such employs

And stir the flames of pure romance—

That charming, captivating dance

That beguiles all in its golden glow—

And stir its seeds that it may grow

The ones that sprout in bright daylight

The ones that bud within the night

And those that blossom wild and free

As I will, so mote it be

Leave the vase in front of the candle until the wick burns out, then place the vase in a sunny spot in your home. (A bedroom windowsill is ideal.) As the flower opens, so will romance blossom.

Traffic
Quick Incantation to Move Traffic

Sun, I call upon Your power

With Your golden rays, please shower

This road with Your directing light

So this traffic now takes flight

Move it with Your guiding rays

But keep all safely in Your gaze

So none are harmed along the way

But move it fast—just as I say!

7

Noon: Father Sun Efforts

Even though logic would dictate that all spells in this section be performed at noon, you have a little more leeway when working with the energies of the Father Sun. In fact, great success may be obtained when working these efforts any time between the hours of 11:00 a.m. and 1:00 p.m.

Balance
Rune Spell

Materials

1 white candle

Mistletoe oil (for instructions, please see
    Wishing Rune Spell in the Dawn section)

Begin by inscribing the following rune (figure 15) on the candle. (This rune is a combination of Gifu, Wunjo, and Tyr, and brings wishes, joy, and balance.)

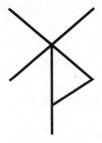

Figure 15: Combination Rune of Gifu, Wunjo, and Tyr

Anoint the candle with the oil, and visualize yourself as being in perfect balance with all the aspects of your life—physical, emotional, mental, and spiritual. Light the candle and watch how the flame balances perfectly as it burns the wick. Then place your hands loosely around the candle and say something like:

Rune that's bound with all things good

Let this wish be understood:

I ask for balance in all things

The joy and pleasure that it brings

True calm of spirit, real peace of mind

The flexibility that's hard to find

Within the busy life I lead

Binding rune, now intercede

And bring to me the things I ask

I conjure you unto this task

Let the candle burn out, and know that balance is on the way.

Business Success
Success/Money Draw Oil Spell

Materials

¼ cup olive oil, extra virgin

1 tablespoon basil, dried

1 teaspoon orange peel, dried

¼ teaspoon frankincense resin, powdered

9 dimes

1 small piece of aventurine

Bottle with tight-fitting lid

Food processor or blender

Place the oil, basil, orange peel, and frankincense resin in a food processor or blender and process on high for a minute or two. Place the dimes and the stone in the bottle, and pour the oil mixture on top. Then cap the bottle, shake it well, and enchant the oil by saying something like:

Herbs and stone and coins of power

And Father Sun at peak of power

Meld and mix Your energies

Into this oil and bring to me

Success in business—bring it fast—

In quantities that flabbergast

And bring the cash related, too

Do now what I ask of You

So that when this oil's applied

My success is amplified

Place the bottle where the Sun's noontime rays shine upon it, and leave it there until 1:00 p.m. the next day. Apply the oil to the doorknobs of your establishment, the threshold of your front door, your mailbox, your cash register, and any business cash you have on hand. If you don't have a store front, anoint yourself with a bit of the oil daily. (This is also a good oil for anointing green candles to draw money.)

Childbirth
Raphael Seal Spell

Materials

1 purple candle

1 seal of Raphael (duplicate figure 16 with
    a scanner or copy machine, then cut it out)

1 tablespoon lavender, dried

Charcoal block

Light the candle and the charcoal block. As they burn, write the name of the pregnant woman on the back of the seal. Hold the seal between your hands in a "praying" position, with your thumbs touching your chest, and visualize an easy childbirth that produces a healthy baby. Then place the seal on the charcoal, design up, and scatter the lavender on top. Ask the assistance of Raphael and Father Sun by saying something like:

Raphael and Father Sun

Smile on (name of person) 'til this is done

Let this baby come with ease

Protect them both, I ask You, please

From all amount of harm and ill

And in them both, please now instill

The power of Your love and might

Let it replace all pain and fright

So that the coming of this perfect treasure

Is remembered with both joy and pleasure

I ask You both to hear my plea

And do now what I ask of Thee

Figure 16: Seal of Raphael

Let the candle wick burn out, then scatter the ashes in the yard of the pregnant woman.

Compassion
Spell for Understanding

Materials
1 pink candle
1 teaspoon thyme, dried
1 small piece of rose quartz
Pencil
Vegetable oil

Using the pencil, inscribe a heart on the candle with your initials in the center, then anoint the candle with the oil and roll it in the thyme. Light the candle and, holding the rose quartz in your hands, visualize your heart opening to others. See yourself becoming more understanding of their plights and more considerate of their feelings. Then ask Father Sun's assistance by saying something like:

Father Sun, I am Your child
And as such, please reconcile
The problem that I have to feel
What others do; I now appeal
Unto Your warm and golden love
To send compassion from above
And let it seep into my heart

So that its chill will now depart
And empathy will take its place
And consideration and its grace
Will become a valid part of me
As I will, so mote it be

Leave the stone in front of the candle until the wick burns out, then carry the stone with you.

Clarity
Clear Vision Spell

Materials
1 yellow candle
1 small magnifying glass

Light the candle and hold the magnifying glass in your hands. Visualize yourself seeing everything in minute detail exactly as if it were magnified. Then ask the Sun for His illuminating properties by saying something like:

Sun, please help me now to see
That which always escapes me
Illuminate, please, every angle
And with Your rays, please disentangle
All the mess that's in the way
So that I'm not led astray
And as this dancing flame melts wax

Melt all away but just the facts

And guide me as I sort them through

Clear focused vision, I ask of You

Leave the magnifying glass in front of the candle until the wick burns out, then carry the object with you to aid in good decision-making.

Charging
Charging Chant for Tools, Stones, and Other Objects

Hold the tool or object in your hands and offer it to the Father Sun for charging by saying something like:

Father Sun, I ask You lend

Your great power without end

To charge this (name of object) for me

So it will work effectively

Lend to it Your love and light

Your radiance that glows so bright

Infuse it with Your magic touch

And fill it to the brim; as such

It shall retain Your potency

As I will, so mote it be

Leave the tool beneath the Sun's light for at least three hours, then store it as normal.

Deception
Secrets-Be-Gone Spell

Materials
1 yellow candle
¼ teaspoon gold glitter
Vegetable oil

Anoint the candle with the oil, then roll it in the glitter. Light the candle and visualize all deception being swept from your midst, and all relevant information being out in the open. Then ask the assistance of Father Sun by saying something like:

Father Sun, illuminate

What's hidden now and terminate

The need for cloaks and secrecy

Remove them so that I can see

What I should to end this strife

And move forward with my life

Let me see all with clarity

As I will, so mote it be

Let the candle wick burn out and know that all will become clear.

Decision-Making
Reversible Candle Spell

Materials

1 white candle

1 black permanent marker

Pencil

Using the pencil, inscribe a question mark on the candle. Next, color the candle completely—including the top and bottom—with the black marker. Light the candle and visualize yourself finding the right solution and making the best decision for everyone involved. Then ask the Sun's assistance by saying something like:

Father Sun, please help me see

All options open unto me

With Your light, please disentangle

Every choice and every angle

So that alternatives will be

Absolutely clear to me

And having done that, I ask too

That You hold me straight and true

To a decision that is best for all

So that harm won't come to call

On any party that's involved

I ask You, Sun, please help me solve

This quandary that's befallen me

As I will, so mote it be

Let the candle wick burn out.

Eloquence
Quick Speak-Easy Chant

Said before speaking in front of others, this chant alleviates stuttering and other problems that keep your message from hitting its mark.

Father Sun, please shed Your light

Upon my words and make them right

Let them tumble out with ease

Making sense until I cease

To speak; O Father, hear my plea

And do now what I ask of Thee

Family
Family Harmony Spell

Materials

1 apple

Sharp knife

Cut the apple into as many equal pieces as you have family members, and place the pieces where the rays of the midday Sun will shine upon them. Place your hands over the pieces and ask Father Sun for His assistance by saying something like:

Father Sun, shine on us all

And with Your warmth, please now install

A sense of family unity

A growing sense of harmony

And a love that can't be torn

By arguments or squabbles borne

Within its web or at its door

Instill, too, at its very core

A sense humor and real joy

That can never be destroyed

O Father Sun, now hear my plea

And bring these things I ask of Thee

Leave the pieces in place for at least an hour, then cast them into running water to ensure an even flow of love, harmony, and compassion throughout the family.

Home Blessing

Nasties-Be-Gone Spell

Materials

1 quart water, bottled

1 tablespoon angelica

1 tablespoon mistletoe

1 tablespoon rue

1 stick of frankincense incense

1 stick of myrrh incense

1 white candle

1 purple candle

1 red candle

4 copies of the Sun card from the tarot
  (duplicate the card with a scanner or copy
  machine, then cut out)

1 seal of Raphael (duplicate figure 16 with
  a scanner or copy machine, then cut it out)

1 seal of Michael (duplicate figure 17 with
  a scanner or copy machine, then cut it out)

1 seal of Gabriel (duplicate figure 18 with
  a scanner or copy machine, then cut it out)

1 seal of Uriel (duplicate figure 19 with a scanner or
copy machine, then cut it out)

Spray bottle

Adhesive tape

Using half of the water, boil the herbs for five minutes, then remove from heat and set aside to cool. Starting at the eastern-most room of your home and moving in a clockwise motion along the perimeter with the lit incense, visualize everything negative being tossed out while chanting something like:

I cast all ill from within this space

It's gone forever from this place

Repeat the process with each room.

Then place the candles in the center of the home and place the seals and the tarot card copies in front of them. Light the white candle, saying:

White light protect and seal
This place from harm, imagined or real

Light the purple candle, saying:

By color of purple, I conjure power
It grows within me by minute and hour

Light the red candle, saying:

By color of red, I take action
Against harmful spirits and their attraction

Starting at the eastern-most point of your home, tape the Raphael seal to the wall, saying something like:

O Raphael of Air and smoke
All negativity now choke
From within these walls and space
I invoke You to protect this place

Going to the southern-most point of your home, tape the Michael seal to the wall, saying something like:

O Michael, with Your sword aflame
Cast out all who seek to maim
Or mar the joy within this space
I invoke You to protect this place

Figure 17: Seal of Michael

Going to the western-most point of your home, tape the Gabriel seal to the wall, saying something like:

O Gabriel, of tides and sea

Cleanse this home of energy

That's harmful; cast it from this space

I invoke You to protect this place

Figure 18: Seal of Gabriel

Going to the northern-most point of your home, tape the Uriel seal to the wall, saying something like:

And Uriel of grounding force

Let harmony within now course

Allow no ill within this space

I invoke You to protect this place

Figure 19: Seal of Uriel

Place your hands over the tarot card copies and ask for the Sun's blessing by saying something like:

Great Illuminating Sun Who changes dark to light

Bring Your golden rays now to these walls

And bring to them the bright

Joy for which You're known and Your harmony now, too

Fill each room again with light and give it life anew

I call upon Your aid this day and consecrate this space

To You, O Sun; protect it well and smile upon this place

Starting with the Raphael seal and moving in order, tape a tarot card copy beneath each seal.

Strain the herbs from the tea and pour the mixture into the spray bottle along with the remaining water. Shake the mixture well, saying something like:

Herbs of Sun, now magic potion

I conjure you to cast commotion

Far from these walls and from this space

I conjure you to protect this place

Lightly mist furniture, walls, baseboards, and thresholds with the tea, and pour any leftovers down the drain. Let the candle wicks burn out and bury any leftover wicks or wax.

Justice
The Fair Deal Bath

Materials

5 teaspoons chamomile, dried (5 chamomile teabags may be substituted)

1 quart water

1 quart jar with screw-on lid

Place the chamomile and the water in the quart jar, secure the lid, and take it outdoors at noon. Offer it to Father Sun and ask for His assistance by saying something like:

To You, I offer now this tea

A tool toward justice, let it be

I ask Your golden rays peruse

Its properties and then infuse

It with Your warmth until it's blessed

And Your power manifests

To bring swift justice unto me

As I will, so mote it be

Leave the jar outdoors until dusk, then strain out the herbs and add the tea to your bath water. Completely immerse yourself five times while visualizing a fair resolution to the problem at hand. Allow the water on your body to dry naturally.

Knowledge Retention
Lily of the Valley Spell

Materials

1 glass bulb forcing container (readily available
   at garden centers and arts and crafts stores)

1 small piece of fluorite

1 lily of the valley bulb

Small rocks for the container

Water

Place the rocks in the container with the fluorite on top. Then fill the container with water, and add the bulb. Place your hands over the bulb and visualize your

memory improving as the bulb sprouts and grows.
Then enchant it by saying something like:

> *Lily of the Valley, grow*
>
> *As you root and sprout, bestow*
>
> *New roots in knowledge unto me*
>
> *So I retain all that I see*
>
> *And everything I hear as well*
>
> *And as you bloom into white bells*
>
> *My memory shall blossom, too*
>
> *So all the knowledge I've accrued*
>
> *Will surface quickly on demand*
>
> *Any time at my command*
>
> *O Precious Bulb, now bring to me*
>
> *What I will; so mote it be*

Place the container in a sunny spot, and keep the water
reservoir full.

Legal Matters
Victory Charm Bag

Materials

½ teaspoon marigold, dried

½ teaspoon John the Conqueror, dried

1 sheet beeswax with wick (readily available
   at arts and crafts stores)

1 small piece of sunstone

1 yellow drawstring bag or yellow handkerchief

The day before your court date, spread the herbs evenly across the beeswax sheet. Then, placing the wick at the top edge, tightly roll the sheet toward you to form a candle. Light the candle, and visualize a favorable ruling. Hold the stone in your hand, and offer it to Father Sun by saying something like:

Father Sun, I am Your child

And as such, I ask You smile

Upon me as I go to court

Please be my strength and my support

Infuse this stone that's named for You

With Your magic through and through

So that it brings me more than luck

When the gavel's blow is struck

Father Sun, a victory

Is what I ask; so mote it be

Place the stone in the bag or in the center of the handkerchief, and leave it in front of the candle until the candle wick burns out. Collect the burned wick and any leftover wax and add it to the bag or handkerchief. Secure the contents well, and carry the parcel with you to court.

Lost Objects
Illumination Chant

This chant works wonders for lost keys, paperwork, or anything else that's been misplaced.

Father Sun, with bright light shine

On this thing I cannot find

Work with true expediency

Illuminate it immediately

And bring it forth at once to me

As I will, so mote it be

Magical Power
Boost My Power Chant

Father Sun, now at Your peak

Bring the power that I seek

Give it life and make it strong

So the magic that I long

For manifests with swiftest ease

As I will, so mote it be

Marriage
Happy Union Charm

Materials

1 red candle

1 pink candle

6 ivy leaves with stems

2 feet ¼-inch burgundy satin ribbon

2 feet ¼-inch pink satin ribbon

1 3-inch gold-colored metal ring (available at
   arts and crafts stores)

Glue (optional)

Using the flame of a match or a cigarette lighter, melt a bit of wax on the side of one of the candles, then press the two together to join them. Light the wicks and visualize the relationship being a happy one for its duration. Hold the ribbons together as one and, leaving a twelve-inch tail, secure them to the ring with a knot. Place the stem of one ivy leaf at the top of the ring (the stem should be pointing toward the left) and secure it by wrapping the ribbon tightly around it and the ring, continuing to wrap until the stem is completely covered. As you wrap, chant something like:

Ivy, ribbon, golden ring

Happiness to us, please bring

In this life we've joined together

Keep us far from stormy weather

Working clockwise and spacing evenly, continue to chant, add leaves, and wrap the ring with ribbon, securing with glue if necessary. When all the leaves are in place and the ring is completely wrapped, secure the end with a knot and tie the ends in a bow. Place the wreath in front of the candles and say something like:

Father Sun, now hear my plea

Please smile upon my love and me

Bring to us Your joy and light

And lend Your passion to each night

To our kisses, add Your fire

With Your flame, stoke our desire

With happiness, please fill our hearts

So that as each new morning starts

Our joy and pleasure starts anew

From honest hearts whose love is true

I ask You, too, infuse this charm

With protection from all harm

So as we build this life as one

Our bliss remains 'til it is done

Leave the charm in front of the candles until the wicks burn out, then hang the wreath over the bed.

Protection
Watch My Back Prayer

Visualize the rays of the Sun wrapping themselves around you to create a golden bubble that keeps you safe from harm. Then ask the protection of Father Sun by saying something like:

Father Sun, protect my back

Keep me safe from all attack

Be it visible or unseen

I ask You now to intervene

With all Your magic and Your power

Protect me now from where You tower

Secure me with Your rays of gold

Wrap me in Your arms and hold

Me tightly until danger's spent

And I am free of ill intent

Father Sun, now hear my plea

As I will, so mote it be

Research

Information Illumination Spell

Materials

1 yellow candle

9 cloves, whole

Paper and pen

Fireproof dish

Light the candle, and while it burns, write the following chant on a piece of paper. Hold the paper in your hands and visualize yourself finding the exact information that you need. When the image is firmly fixed in your mind's eye, say the chant to Father Sun with feeling.

> *Father Sun, now shine Your light*
>
> *On what I need, both bold and bright*
>
> *Lead me to the proper tools*
>
> *Whether common, scarce, or miniscule*
>
> *And guide me toward reliable*
>
> *Sources and verifiable*
>
> *Information for my work*
>
> *Shine on all so nothing lurks*
>
> *Within the shadows or escapes*
>
> *Me due to diverse form or shape*
>
> *Father Sun, now hear my plea*
>
> *Do now what I ask of Thee*

Place the cloves in the center of the paper one at a time, saying with each:

> *Clove of knowledge, bring to me*
> *What I need; so mote it be*

Then fold the paper in half three times to secure the cloves, and light the paper from the flame of the candle. Set it in the fireproof dish and let it burn to ash. When the candle wick burns out, scatter the ashes outdoors as close to your home as possible.

Study
Fact Retention Chant

Materials
Textbook or notes in question

Place your hands over the book or notes you need to study, and ask Father Sun for assistance by saying something like:

> *Father Sun, both bold and bright*
> *Upon these pages, shed Your light*
> *Illuminate the knowledge here*
> *So all I see is crystal clear*
> *And all the facts stay in my head*
> *Let me retain all I have read*

Study as usual, and know that everything you read will stay with you.

Success
Sachiel Success Spell

Materials
1 yellow candle

1 blue candle

1 tablespoon sandalwood chips (you may
substitute loose sandalwood incense)

1 sheet paper

Green pen

Charcoal block

Censer or fireproof dish with sand

Gather the materials on a Thursday, placing the censer in front of you, the yellow candle to its left, and the blue candle to its right. Then write your wish for success on the paper. (It's important to be specific here. If you're working this effort for general success, write "general success" on the page. If you're looking for success in a specific endeavor, though, word your wish accordingly.)

Light the yellow candle, saying something like:

By strongest light on Thursday blessed

My desires now manifest

Light the charcoal block and sprinkle half the sandalwood on it. Then light the blue candle and invoke the angel Sachiel by saying something like:

Sachiel, now come to me

And bring success along with Thee

See what's written on this page

And my desire, please now engage

So that it quickly manifests

Without trial or undue tests

And, Sachiel, please guide me, too

So that all mundane follow-through

Toward this success is clear to me

As I will, so mote it be

Place the remaining sandalwood on top of the paper, and fold it several times to secure. Light the paper from the flame of the blue candle, and place it on top of the charcoal block to burn. Let the candles burn out, and toss the ashes on the winds.

Theft
Thief Repellent Spell

Materials

1 white candle

1 seal of Raphael (duplicate figure 16 with
    a scanner or copy machine, then cut it out)

1 seal of Michael (duplicate figure 17 with
    a scanner or copy machine, then cut it out)

1 seal of Gabriel (duplicate figure 18 with
    a scanner or copy machine, then cut it out)

1 seal of Uriel (duplicate figure 19 with
    a scanner or copy machine, then cut it out)

Vanilla oil
Red pen
Adhesive tape

Anoint the candle with the oil and light the wick. Then write your address and the name of each person who lives with you on the back of each seal. Moisten your index finger with a few drops of oil and, starting at the upper right-hand corner and moving in a clockwise manner, use it to anoint each corner on the back of each seal. Turn the seals right-side up and place them in front of the candle. Then ask the archangels' assistance by saying something like:

Raphael, now hear my plea

Protect this home from thievery

Michael, too, I call to task

From all theft, our things now mask

Gabriel, I call to You

Keep all here safe from theft now, too

And Uriel, please come as well

Keep thieves away by rhyme of spell

Archangels four, protect us all

And our things; let us not fall

Victim to unsavory

Characters or thievery

Archangels four, I conjure Thee

To this task; so mote it be

Leave the seals in front of the candle until the wick burns out. Then, starting at the east, tape the Raphael seal to the point where the wall and ceiling meet. Repeat the process, taping the Michael seal to the south, the Gabriel seal to the west, and the Uriel seal to the north.

Truth
Sunstone Charm

Materials

1 white candle

1 small piece of blue sunstone

Light the candle and hold the stone in your hands while visualizing those around you being forced to tell the truth, regardless of the circumstances. Then offer the stone to the Sun by saying something like:

O Father Sun, of brightest light

You who bring the day from night

I ask You to bring the truth to light

So nothing's hidden from my sight

Or from my ears; now bring it forth

From east and west and south and north

O Father Sun, now hear my plea

And do just what I ask of Thee

Leave the stone in front of the candle until the wick burns out, then carry the stone with you when truth is at issue.

8

Afternoon:
Sage/Warrior Sun Efforts

The general period for working the spells in this section is between approximately 1:00 p.m. and 3:00 p.m. Unless otherwise specified, those spells that utilize the energy of the Warrior Sun tend to be most successful when performed during the first hour of this time-frame, while those pertaining to the Sage Sun enjoy more success when performed during the latter. Efforts that invoke both phases, however, may be performed at any time during the period.

Business Marketing Strategies
Make It Saleable Spell

Materials

1 orange candle

½ teaspoon cinnamon

½ teaspoon sage, dried

1 dollar bill

1 small piece of orange calcite

Picture or sketch of the product to be marketed

Green embroidery floss
Vegetable oil

Anoint the candle with the oil, then roll it in a mixture of cinnamon and sage. Light the wick and hold the picture in your hands. Visualize yourself coming up with the perfect marketing solution—one that will not only sell your product, but will set it apart from that of your competition. Continue to visualize, seeing customers lining up to purchase your product, enjoying its benefits, and extolling its wonders to other people. When the image is fixed firmly in your mind's eye, place the picture face up in front of the candle and lay the dollar bill on top. Hold your hands over the dollar and ask the assistance of the Warrior Sun by saying something like:

From sketch to cash is what I ask

O hearken, Warrior, to this task

Lend to me Your strategies

So this product moves with ease

Let all angles come to mind—

Those to which I have been blind—

And replace brain fog with clarity

As I will, so mote it be

Hold the piece of calcite in your hands and see the marketing strategies being amplified to the point that it's difficult to keep up with supply and demand. Hold the image for a few moments, and then place the stone on top of the dollar, saying something like:

Orangest stone of amplification
Bring to this spell your magnification
Join your powers with the Sun
Until the task at hand is done
To amplify both strategy
And sales is what I ask of thee
Lend your help at once to me
As I will, so mote it be

Fold the picture around the dollar and the stone to make a square or rectangular parcel, then wrap the parcel with the embroidery floss from top to bottom and side to side, and tie it securely with a knot, saying something like:

By greenest floss and knot of one
This spell is cast; so be it done

Leave the parcel in front of the candle. While the candle burns, set to work on advertising and marketing ideas. When the wick burns out, place the parcel in close proximity to the product paperwork—in the file itself is a good idea—and leave it there to do its job.

Business Partnerships
Do Your Part Spell

Materials

1 black candle

¼ teaspoon chili powder

¼ teaspoon ginger

¼ teaspoon sage, dried

1 jet pendant or jet bead

Small key ring

Vegetable oil

Combine the herbs and anoint the candle with the oil, then roll the candle in the herbal mixture, and light the wick. Hold the jet in your hand and visualize your business partner picking up the slack and handling his or her part of the work. See all of the problems flying out the window, everyone involved being more relaxed, and the business running smoothly. Once the image is firmly fixed in your mind's eye, ask the Sage/Warrior Sun for His assistance by saying something like:

O Warrior Sun, I call to You

The battle's on—there's work to do

I call to You, Sage Sun, as well

For Your wisdom in this spell

Bring some balance in our work

Let not (name of partner) his/her duties shirk

See that she/he no longer slacks

And that his/her performance does not lack

The diligence that is required
See that she/he becomes inspired
Toward productivity once more
O Sage and Warrior, I implore
You to infuse this piece of jet
With Your strengths and in it set
A call to true efficiency
As I will, so mote it be

Slip the pendant or bead onto the key ring and leave it in front of the candle until the wick burns out, then give the key ring to your partner.

Contracts
Get a Contract Spell

Materials
1 red candle
1 purple candle
2 teaspoons basil, dried
Paperwork for the contract in question
Vegetable oil

Anoint the candles with the oil and roll them in the basil. Place the paperwork—this could be an application, a query letter, an ad, or even a flyer you hope will bring you a contract—between the candles and light the wicks. Visualize yourself receiving the contract and getting the deal of your dreams. When the image is firmly fixed in your mind's eye, turn the papers face down, lick your index finger, and use it to mark each page with a quartered circle while saying something like:

By the power of the Warrior Sun
This contract's mine; so be it done

Once all the pages are marked, leave them face down between the candles. When the wicks burn out, submit the paperwork, place the ad, distribute the flyers, or tend to whatever other mundane steps are necessary to set things in motion.

Financial Balance
Debt-Be-Gone Spell

Materials
1 black candle
½ lemon
Copies of your bills
Fireproof dish

Tally the amount of your bills and inscribe the candle with the total. Then use the lemon to anoint the candle and light the wick. Hold the copies of your bills in your hand, and visualize the amounts decreasing until you're virtually debt free. Allow the worry to evaporate, and feel the relief. Then call on the Sage/Warrior Sun for assistance by saying something like:

As bills come in and cash goes out
Financial balance, bring about

Lend Your guidance now to me

And direct my steps 'til I'm debt free

Banish bills—relieve all woe—

Destroy all blocks so cash can flow

With interest and with dividends

Bring all debts now to an end

Bring what I ask at once to me

As I will, so mote it be

Light the copies one by one from the flame of the candle and let each burn to ash in the dish. When the candle wick burns out, scatter the ashes on the winds.

Goal Achievement
Life Mapping Spell

Materials

1 sheet white paper

1 yellow candle

Pen or pencil

On the paper, draw a personal "life map" with the date of your birth in the lower left-hand corner, the present date close to the center, and the goal most close to your heart in the upper right-hand corner. Then use the space between the present date and your goal to write in the steps necessary to achieve what you wish along with the realistic timeframes.

When you're satisfied with the map, place it in front of the candle. Light the candle, place your hands over the map, and say something like:

I call on You, Sage/Warrior Sun

To aid me 'til this goal is won

Lend strategy and common sense

Help me to see that which prevents

My goal from being manifest

And lend Your strength with every test

I must endure to reach my aim

Illuminate, please, with Your flame

The most direct route to my goal

I conjure You unto this role:

To guide me 'til this goal is won

I call on You, Sage/Warrior Sun

Visualize yourself accomplishing the task outlined on the map, then leave the paper in front of the candle until the wick burns out. Hang the map in a spot where you'll see it every day.

Leadership
Chant for Guidance, Direction, and Courage

O Warrior/Sage, now hear my plea

And lend Your powers unto me

Guide my steps, direct my views

So all solutions I peruse

Bring fairness to all judgment calls

So I may do my best for all

And when I find myself in doubt

Please lend the strength to sit things out

Until the answer becomes clear

And help me to dispel the fears

Of those that I'm compelled to lead

I ask You, too, O Sun, to breed

Courage, kindness, laughter, joy

Within my heart; help me employ

All Your strengths as I escort

My charges; grant me Your support

Problem Solving
Prism Spell

Materials

1 white candle

1 teaspoon sage, powdered

1 small crystal prism

Vegetable oil

Anoint the candle with the oil, then roll it in the sage. Light the candle and say something like:

Wax and sage with flame so bright

Guide me now with perfect light

Hold the prism in front of the flame so it catches the light. Take note of the angles of the object and pay attention to the rainbows it casts on the walls. Spend a few minutes thinking about your problem and how, like the prism, it's multifaceted. Then, turning the prism around and around, ask the assistance of the Sage Sun by saying something like:

Wisest Sun, now hear my call

As these rainbows grace the wall

Help me see each angle well

Every facet and each cell

Of this problem that I face

Bring me quickly to its base

Illuminate the best solution

And bring about quick resolution

Meditate for a few minutes on the many facets of the prism while studying the problem, then leave the prism in front of the candle until the wick burns out, knowing that a solution will come. Whenever another problem arises, use the prism as a meditation device.

Protection
Chant to the Warrior Sun

Warrior Sun, now be my shield

Your strength and power, quickly wield

Wrap me in Your arms so strong

And hold me there 'til danger's gone

And with Your sword, protect me well

All harm and danger, now dispel

Hearken, Warrior Sun, to me

As I will, so mote it be

Visualize the rays of the Sun wrapping around you and completely enveloping you in a golden bubble that nothing can penetrate.

Strength
Spell to Get Through a Bad Situation

Materials

1 red seven-day candle

5 bay leaves

1 red charm bag or red handkerchief

1 small piece of bloodstone

Paper and pen

Charcoal block

Censer or fireproof dish

Begin by drawing a picture of the Sun in the center of the paper, then draw a sword on top of the Sun. Place the drawing beneath the candle and light the wick, saying something like:

By flame of wick in wax so red

By sharpest blade that all foes dread

By Warrior Sun of strength and might

I cast a spell of growing light

Light the charcoal block, and hold the bay leaves in your hand while seeing yourself getting through the ordeal at hand swiftly and expediently. Hold the image for a few moments, then place the bay leaves on the charcoal one at a time, saying with each:

> *As you smolder on the fire*
>
> *Ignite the strength that I desire*
>
> *And as you burn to ash and cinder*
>
> *Courage to me also render*

Then hold the stone in your hand and offer it to the Warrior Sun, saying something like:

> *O Warrior Sun, please grant me strength*
>
> *That I may endure this burden's length*
>
> *Bring to me Your courage, too*
>
> *In this thing that I must do*
>
> *Let my steps not falter, please*
>
> *Guide them swiftly and with ease*
>
> *And let this trial that's come to pass*
>
> *Go quickly so it does not last*
>
> *Longer than it should for me*
>
> *But while it does, I ask of Thee*
>
> *Infuse this stone with what I've asked*
>
> *So it aids me in this task*
>
> *O Warrior Sun, now hear my plea*
>
> *And do as I command of Thee*

Place the stone in the bag and leave it in front of the candle. When the wick burns out, fold the drawing and add it to the bag. Carry the bag with you until the ordeal passes.

Travel
Safe Travel Prayer

Sun Who travels through the sky
I ask that You now cast Your eye
Upon me as I venture out
Regardless of my choice of route
Keep me both safe and secure
And I ask that You assure
That luggage arrives expediently
At the places it should be
With no mishaps for it or me
As I will, so mote it be

Victory
Winner's Circle Spell

Materials
1 purple candle
1 teaspoon sage, powdered
1 bay leaf
Pen

Charcoal block
Vegetable oil
Censer or fireproof dish

Anoint the candle with the oil, then roll it in the sage. Light the candle and visualize the flame lighting your way to victory. Then write the subject matter of the effort at hand on the bay leaf. (Keep this simple but specific. If it's a competition, write the name of the game. If it's a court case, write the docket number or the name of the case. You get the idea.) Burn the bay leaf on the charcoal, and invoke the powers of the Sage/Warrior Sun by saying something like:

Warrior Sun—and Sage Sun, too—
Hear me as I call to You
I ask Your wisdom and foresight
As I embark upon this fight
And I ask of You, as well
To lend that at which You excel:
The tactical knowledge and strategy
That will ensure my victory
As I embrace this grueling test
I conjure You to manifest
All these things within my core
And, as well, just one thing more:
Push me toward the final goal—
The winner's circle—play the role

Of Aids unto my victory
As I will, so mote it be

As the leaf burns, visualize your certain victory. Let the candlewick burn out.

War
Prayer To Keep a Soldier Safe

Warrior Sun, up in the sky
I ask that You now cast Your eye
Upon (name of soldier) now at war
And keep him/her under the radar
Of Your watch and in Your sight
Grant his/her safety day and night
And when she/he feels a sense of dread
Help him/her calmly use his/her head
Grant him/her mental safety, too
And bring to him/her an avenue
To relieve emotional stress
And prevent undue duress
'Til his/her mission is complete
And once again, she/he feels the sweet
And warm embrace of his/her loved ones
Far from the sounds of war and guns
This I ask You, Warrior Sun
As I will, so be it done

Wisdom
Invocation for Wisdom

O Wisest Sun, I know as Sage

Grant the wisdom of Your age

Help me pick my battles well

Help me look at every cell

Of situations that arise

And find solutions that apply

Show me well when I should speak

And when such voice would only wreak

More havoc; let me know as well

When to listen to compel

The best solution for all those

Involved and caught within the throes

Of problems. And I ask You, too

To help me sort all issues through

So no decision that I make

Brings the sting of true heartache

To any who might be concerned

Guide me well that I may learn

The timeless wisdom of Your age

Teach me well, O Wisest Sage

9

Sunset: Grandfather/ Sacrificial Sun Efforts

The general period for working the spells in this section is between 3:00 p.m. and Sunset. Unless otherwise specified, those spells that utilize the energy of the Grandfather Sun tend to be most successful when performed until approximately an hour before Sunset, while those pertaining to the Sacrificial Sun enjoy more success when performed thereafter. Efforts that invoke both phases, however, may be performed at any time during the period.

Abuse
Samael Sigil Spell

(Abuse is a serious matter. Please take whatever mundane steps are necessary—calling the police or filing a complaint come to mind here—before performing this spell.)

Materials

1 red candle

1 sigil of Samael (duplicate figure 20 with
    a scanner or copy machine, then cut it out)

1 teaspoon allspice

Vegetable oil

Anoint the candle with oil, then roll it in the allspice.
Light the candle, and hold the sigil in your hands while
visualizing Samael coming to your aid. Invoke the
archangel by saying something like:

Samael, Who stands against

Abusive people who bring angst

To others with their power trips

Guard me now against the grips

Of (name of person) and his/her cruel abuse

And use Your sword to cut me loose

From his/her clutches immediately

I ask You, Samael, to set me free

And set me on a safe new path

And, Samael, in the aftermath

Keep me safely in Your sight

Protect me, too, with all Your might

So of abuse, I'm truly free

As I will, so mote it be

Leave the sigil in front of the candle until the wick burns
out, then carry the sigil with you as a protective device.

Figure 20: Sigil of Samael

Addiction

Spell Against Self-Destructive Tendencies

(This spell is only designed to handle minor addictions and cravings; treatment of serious disorders should be handled by a qualified healthcare practitioner.)

Materials
1 purple candle
1 small piece of moonstone
1 seal of Gabriel (duplicate figure 18 with
   a scanner or copy machine, then cut it out)
2 4-inch squares of silver or white fabric
Myrrh or jasmine oil
Needle and thread

Anoint the candle with the oil, then rub a bit of the oil on the moonstone. Place the seal in the center of one fabric square and place the stone on top, then set it in front of the candle. Place the other fabric square on top. Hold your hands over the fabric, and visualize yourself living a life that's free from cravings and self-destructive tendencies. Then call on the archangel Gabriel for assistance by saying something like:

I call upon You, Gabriel

You Who know my problems well

You Who understand my weakness

My flaws, my faults, and sees the bleakness

That pervades my spirit now

Come to me and please endow

Me with Your courage and Your might

Stand beside me; help me fight

Against this self-destructive urge

And with Your power, help me purge

It from my life once and for all

And as the Dying Sun does fall

From the sky and sinks below

Earth's horizon, send this foe

Along with Him unto its death

Let it not draw another breath;

And fill my spirit, too, with hope

So I can see the very scope

Of what my life can truly be

I call You, Gabriel! Come to me!

Sew the edges of the fabric together to secure the seal and stone, then leave it in front of the candle until the wick burns out. Carry the pouch with you, and hold it whenever you feel addictive urges start to surface.

Anger
Amethyst Bath Spell

Materials

1 gallon bottled water

1 small piece of amethyst

Take the water and amethyst outdoors during Sunset and, facing west, drop the stone into the water container. Watch the Sun cast its fading rays on the container, and visualize your anger dying with His final light. Then place your hands around the container and enchant it by saying something like:

Life-giving waters and amethyst

I call on you now to assist

In choking out this angry fire

Work together and conspire

To contain and cool its rage

To squelch its flames and disengage

It forever from my life

And wash away all stress and strife;

Lend your calming peace to smooth

My ruffled feathers, and then soothe

Me with your pure serenity

As I will, so mote it be

Leave the container there for at least one hour, then add the water to your bath. Carry the stone with you, and caress it when you feel a burst of anger coming on.

Anxiety
Anti-Panic Spell

Materials
1 yellow candle
1 teaspoon lavender, dried
1 seal of Raphael (duplicate figure 16 with
   a scanner or copy machine, then cut it out)
Vegetable oil

Anoint the candle in the vegetable oil, then roll it in the lavender. Light the candle and, holding the seal in your hands, visualize anxiety and panic flying right out the window. Then call on the archangel Raphael to complete the job by saying something like:

O Raphael, now come to me

And sweep away anxiety

And all the panic that I feel

When things become less than ideal

Help me now to cope with change

And help me learn to rearrange

My plans with ease and without worry

(Sans the fear that comes with hurry)

So I handle all without alarm,

Nervous tension or fear of harm

O Raphael, please stand by me

And make my life now worry-free

Leave the seal in front of the candle until the wick burns out, then carry the seal with you.

Bad Luck

To Reverse a Run of Bad Luck

Materials

1 white candle

1 4-inch square of purple cloth

1 small piece of black onyx

1 teaspoon thyme

Black permanent marker

Begin by inscribing the candle with the rune shown in figure 21—it's Fehe, the rebirthing rune—then completely color the candle, including the top and bottom, with the marker. Light the wick and place the cloth square in front of it. Holding the stone in your dominant hand, charge it with the power of separation. Visualize the stone growing in size and changing in shape until it forms a fence that keeps all misfortune away from you. Then enchant it by saying something like:

O Blackest Stone of separation

Form a line of demarcation

Between me and this run of luck

Fence off all that runs amuck

And keep it far away from me

As I will, so mote it be

Place the stone in the center of the cloth, then sprinkle it with the thyme while saying something like:

Herb of happiness and change

I conjure you now to exchange

The fortune that has been my bane

For the sort of luck that brings true gain

Tie the four corners of the cloth together to form a pouch. Then, holding it in both hands, call on the angel Cassiel to complete the task and to protect you from further misfortune by saying something like:

O Cassiel, hear my command

Be my Protector; take a stand

Against ill luck that comes my way

Be a shield—keep it at bay—

Cassiel, now hear my plea

Do now what I ask of Thee

Figure 21: Rune of Fehe

Visualize Cassiel shielding you from bad luck, then place the pouch in front of the candle and leave it there until the wick burns out. Carry the pouch with you.

Cleansing

Smudging Spell for Home, Tools, Stones, or Jewelry

Materials

1 tablespoon dragon's blood resin

1 tablespoon frankincense resin

1 tablespoon myrrh resin

Charcoal block

Censer or fireproof dish with sand

Place the charcoal block in the censer or fireproof dish, and light it. Then combine the resins while chanting something like:

> *Resins, mix your energies*
>
> *To cast out negativity*
>
> *So that when on the block you burn*
>
> *All but joy shall cease to churn*

Then, evoking the power of the Sacrificial Sun and using your hand to direct the smoke, burn a little resin at a time on the charcoal block while saying something like:

> *Aging Sacrificial Sun*
>
> *One Who dies when day is done*

Take all nasties with Your light

Banishment, please expedite

So as twilight comes to call

And the darkness starts to fall

All negativity is swept away

I conjure You: Do as I say

Continue to chant until the object or home is completely smudged.

Depression
Depression Eradication Prayer

O Setting Sun of Aging Light

Hearken now unto my plight

Take depression as You go

Take all sadness and all woe

Away from me and hold it tight

So it dies within Your waning light

And as the twilight comes to call

And stars sparkle brightly, one and all

Fill me with Your love so rare

For though You're hidden, You are there

Dieting
Knot Spell for Weight Loss

Materials
Length of black embroidery floss cut to
the size of your waist

Take the floss outdoors as the Sun begins to set, and
spend a moment or two thinking about the things that
keep you from losing the excess weight. Then tie nine
evenly spaced knots in the floss, saying with each:

First knot:

> *By knot of one, I now ignite*
> *A reduction in my appetite*

Second knot:

> *By knot of two, my metabolism*
> *Becomes an active mechanism*

Third knot:

> *By knot of three, I bind desire*
> *For unhealthy foods; it now expires*

Fourth knot:

> *By knot of four, I bind the urge*
> *To binge and gobble, gorge and splurge*

Fifth knot:

> *By knot of five, inertia goes*
> *And exercise, I don't oppose*

Sixth knot:

> *By knot of six, all excess weight*
> *Is bound to quickly dissipate*

Seventh knot:

> *By knot of seven, I resist*
> *Servings larger than two fists*

Eighth knot:

> *By knot of eight, insecurity goes*
> *Self-worth buds and blooms and grows*

Ninth knot:

> *By knot of nine, I bind setbacks*
> *So I stay easily on track*

Finally, tie the two ends together while visualizing yourself reaching your goal weight easily and painlessly. Say something like:

> *By final knot, I set this spell*
> *So each and every single cell*
> *Of my body and my mind*
> *Works together now to bind*
> *Me to this weight-loss strategy*
> *And a healthy ideology*
> *Until of excess pounds I'm free*
> *As I will, so mote it be*

Wear the cord around your neck for the duration of your weight-loss program. (It's okay to wind it double or triple to keep it from getting in your way.)

Enemies

Stay Away From Me Spell

Materials

1 black candle

1 teaspoon salt

1 teaspoon vegetable oil

1 chicken feather or a feather from any
   mild-mannered bird (sparrows, chickadees,
   and wrens are good choices)

Small dish

Light the candle and in a small dish mix the salt with the oil. Hold the feather in your hands and see your enemy fleeing far away from you. Then call upon the setting Sun by saying something like:

O Setting Sun, with dying breath

I ask You take now with Your death

The annoyances that (name of person) doles out

The aggravations that she/he touts

The nastiness she/he likes to peddle

And all the ways she/he tends to meddle

And kill now, too, the urgency

With which she/he feels the need to be

Involved within my life; I ask

Too, that you move him (her) far away

From me—right now—this very day

So of each other, we are free

As I will, so mote it be

Leave the feather and oil mixture in front of the candle until the wick burns out. Dip the feather in the oil and use it to draw a boundary line across your threshold, then leave the feather as close as possible to your enemy's property. (If the enemy is a coworker, dispose of the feather in his or her trash can.)

Fear
Slam the Door Spell

Materials
1 black candle
Paper and pen
Fireproof dish

Light the candle, then write down precisely what you fear, no matter how silly it seems. Using the candle flame, set the paper on fire and let it burn to ash in the fireproof dish. As it burns, say something like:

By Ancient Sun and Elements

I steal the power that Fear once

Had over me; I steal its life

No longer shall I feel its knife

Of terror deep within my heart
It dies today and cannot thwart
The plans that life's laid out for me
I steal its life and I am free

Then, facing north, see your fear as a big, dark, ugly monster, and slam the door of the Earth Element against it. Say something like:

I slam the door of Earth to you
Your stronghold's gone, so bid adieu
To every grounding energy
That gave you life; so mote it be

Face west, and slam the door of the Water Element, saying something like:

I slam the door of Water now
And moisture bleeds out from your brow
It escapes from every pore
You die of thirst now, dry and sore

Face south, and slam the door of the Fire Element, saying something like:

I slam the door of Fire and flame
Passion shrivels and I claim
Your energy—each single shred—
I suck it from you 'til you're dead

Face east, and slam the door of the Air Element, saying something like:

And now, I slam the door of Air
You cannot breathe—you choke and swear—
And as you struggle to draw breath
I laugh out loud now at your death

Finally, stand in the center and slam the door on Akasha, saying something like:

Akasha slams its door now, too
So your spirit dies with you
And as I hear your final hiss
I know you've ceased now to exist

Let the candlewick burn out, and flush the ashes down the toilet.

Gossip
Shut Your Mouth Spell

Materials
Paper and pen
Black marker
Fireproof dish

Start by writing the offender's name on the paper, and drawing a pair of lips below the name. Think about all the nasty things that issue from his or her mouth, then, using the marker, draw a big, black *X* through the lips. Say something like:

No more gossip shall you speak
Your nasty words shall cease to eke

Out from your tongue—they're held within

Where they can't harm or do me in—

I shut your mouth now with this spell

To nastiness; all you can tell

Are lovely things of mine and me

As I will, so mote it be

Burn the paper in the fireproof dish, and flush the ashes down the toilet.

Habits

Bad Habit Destruction Chant

Just as the Sun sinks under the horizon, face west and name your bad habits, one by one. Then ask the Sun to destroy them by saying something like:

O Sacrificial Setting Sun

You Who dies when day is done

Take these habits in Your death

Let them draw not one more breath

Destroy them now with fading light

So as the day sinks into night

Of them, I am finally free

As I will, so mote it be

Know that the Sun has done the job, and take any mundane steps necessary to keep the unsavory characteristics from re-entering your life.

Negative Energy
To Relieve Personal Negativity

Materials

3 sheets of paper (lined, if you like)

White-out

Blue or black pen

Red pen

Green pen

Begin by using a blue or black pen to write down the thoughts running through your head. Do this as quickly as you can. (These don't have to take the form of complete sentences, and the finished result will probably resemble psychobabble.) Don't stop until you've filled all three pages.

Then, using the white-out, paint out all the negative words on the pages. (Any form of "not" or "no" qualifies here.) As you paint through each word, say something like:

By the power of the Dying Sun

Your work here in my life is done

Use the red pen to write positive words where the white-out exists. Change "isn't" to "is," "aren't" to "are," and so forth. As you write each word, say something like:

As the Sun now sinks and dies

Positivity's born—it's on the rise

Now go back through the pages and white-out anything you'd like to change in your life, and make the alteration with the green pen. When you're satisfied with the changes, hold your hands over the pages and say something like:

By death of Sun, I birth anew

A different path and avenue

Where positive changes come to life

Devoid of any stress or strife

And as the Sun is birthed once more

And lights the way to morning's door

These changes start to manifest

And in my life, they are expressed

By rebirthing my reality

As I will, so mote it be

Place the papers where you'll see them every day, and take the appropriate mundane steps toward bringing about positive change.

Nightmares
Dream Catcher Spell

Materials

1 purple candle

3 small pieces of citrine

1 dream catcher

1 2-foot length of yellow ribbon

1 2-foot length of orange ribbon

1 2-foot length of red ribbon

Rubber cement (optional)

Light the candle, then hold the stones in your hand while visualizing them repelling nightmares and other disturbing dreams, and absorbing their residue. Tie one stone into the center of the yellow ribbon, securing it, if necessary, with the glue. Enchant it by saying something like:

> *By power of the Infant Sun*
> *I squash all harm that has been spun*

Tie the ribbon to the center of the left-hand side of the dream catcher's frame. Then tie a stone into the center of the orange ribbon, enchanting it by saying something like:

> *By Father's power and His strength*
> *I repel nightmares at length*

Tie the ribbon to the bottom center of the frame. Then tie the last stone into the center of the red ribbon, and say something like:

> *With dying breath of Ancient Sun*
> *I steal all harm you might have done*

Tie the ribbon to the center right-hand side of the frame. Then, placing the completed dream catcher in front of the candle, say something like:

> *By these phases of the Sun*
> *The magic of this tool is spun*
> *To repel all nastiness*

And absorbing all that might distress

The one who sleeps beneath this tool

From this moment, it shall rule

The dreams that can flow through his/her head

So only pleasantness can tread

The path of sleep; I conjure you:

Bring peaceful resting to him/her, too

So that she/he sleeps throughout the night

Protect him/her with your web of might

Leave the dream catcher in front of the candle until the wick burns out, then hang it above the bed. Once each month, clear the negativity from the tool by leaving it outdoors in the Sun all day.

Obstacles
Sand Spell

Materials

A handful of sand or dry dirt

Holding the sand in your hand, face the setting Sun and ask His assistance by saying something like:

Ancient Sun, with Your last breath

Send obstacles now to their death

Destroy all fences, break all locks,

Rid me of all stumbling blocks

Bring them all to swift demise

So they can no longer rise

And hold me back from what I need

Or my ability to succeed

Crumble them just as this dust

So I move onward as I must

Turn in a counterclockwise circle three times, while seeing obstacles being reduced to nothingness. Then, facing the Sun again, blow the sand from your hand. Know that the Sun will handle the problem.

Peaceful Separation
Black Onyx Spell

Materials
Small piece of black onyx

Hold the stone in your hands and visualize yourself being peacefully removed from the current situation. See it happening without anger, pain, or harm. Then hold the stone up to the sinking Sun and say something like:

Blackest stone and Dying Sun

Work together now as One

To separate me easily

From this problem peacefully

Let not anger interfere

Nor permeate the atmosphere

Instead, bring space between us both

> *And help us move ahead toward growth*
> *Just burn away the cords that bind,*
> *Sun, as Your final rays decline*
> *And, Stone, absorb all nastiness*
> *Hearken now to this request*
> *End this problem peacefully*
> *As I will, so mote it be*

Carry the stone with you.

Prosperity
Come Back Cash Spell

When paying for something in cash, always break a bill larger than necessary so that you'll get smaller bills back in change. Fold the bills toward you before putting them in your wallet, and money will always flow in your direction.

Psychic Attack
Shielding Spell

Materials

1 purple candle

2 4-inch squares of red fabric

1 sigil of Samael (duplicate figure 20 with
   a scanner or copy machine, then cut it out)

1 small piece of black tourmaline

1 teaspoon hyssop
1 teaspoon lavender
1 teaspoon allspice
Needle and thread

Light the candle and place one fabric square in front of it. Place the sigil in the center of the fabric and the stone on top. Position the other fabric square on top, and sew three sides together to form a pouch. Sprinkle the herbs inside the pouch, and sew up the fourth side.

Hold the pouch in your hands and visualize it absorbing all possible psychic attack. Then call on Samael by saying something like:

> *Samael of Righteous Anger*
> *This is no time for idle languor*
> *I call on You, for this is war*
> *Come now, whether near or far*
> *And fight off all attack on me*
> *As I will, so mote it be*

Once you feel His presence, enchant the pouch by saying something like:

> *Stone and herbs and pouch of red*
> *Absorb and soak up and imbed*
> *Every bit of residue*
> *From attack that might bleed through*
> *Hold it safely—hold it tight—*
> *Hold it firmly with your might*

So that none can bother me

As I will, so mote it be

Leave the pouch in front of the candle until the wick burns out, then carry the pouch with you constantly until you feel the attack is over. Bury the pouch in the ground.

Sexual Abuse
Healing Spell

Materials

½ cup water

1 small piece of goldstone

½ teaspoon patchouli

½ teaspoon slippery elm

A few tears

Jar with screw-on lid

Small bottle with cork or tight-fitting lid

On a Sunday just before Sunset, place the water, tears, stone, and herbs in the jar and cap it tightly. Shake the jar to mix the ingredients while saying something like:

Stone and water, herbs and tears

Mix to wash away my fears

Become a potion that will heal

Every shred of pain I feel

And by the Sacrificial Sun

Work until these deeds are done

Place the jar on the windowsill, or in a spot where it can catch the last rays of the Sun. Then shake the jar at sunset each day for the next nine days while repeating the incantation above.

On the last day—this will be a Tuesday—strain out the herbs and enchant the stone and liquid further by saying something like:

Stone and potion, this is war

I conjure you to heal each scar

To heal each hurt, to heal each fear,

To heal the things that caused each tear

And to protect me from this day

From becoming sexual prey

I conjure you to these tasks at hand

You are at war; heed my command

Remove the stone, pour three tablespoons of the liquid into the bottle, and set aside. Sprinkle the remaining potion across any thresholds leading into your home, and the entries to each room. Anoint your heart chakra daily with the potion in the bottle while saying the chant above, and carry the stone with you.

Unwanted Guests

To Keep Unwanted Guests from Entering the Home

Materials

1 tablespoon cloves (powdered)
1 cup boiling water
1 gallon cold water
Spray bottle

Add the cloves to the boiling water and allow the mixture to steep for twenty minutes. As it steeps, hold your hands over the tea and chant something like:

Setting Sun and joyful spice
And Water that's the Source of Life
Mix and meld Your energies
And brew Your magic in this tea
Grow strong and rich—robust and stout—
Enough to keep those people out
Who are not welcome in my space
I conjure You to shield this place

Say the chant twice more, then mix the tea with the gallon of cold water. Fill the spray bottle with the mixture and, paying careful attention to all doors and thresholds, asperge the home while chanting something like:

Magic, cleansing, shielding spray
Hold unwanted guests at bay

Lock them out and keep them far

Don't let them even leave the car

Shield this place at once for me

As I will, so mote it be

Use any leftover tea to asperge the outside of your home and your yard.

Appendix

Celebratory Drink Recipes

The following recipes are for one drink, unless specified otherwise.

Amaretto Sour

1½ ounces amaretto
¾ ounce lemon juice
Maraschino cherry
Orange slice
Crushed ice

Pour amaretto and lemon juice over ice and shake well. Strain into glass and garnish with cherry and orange slice.

Bahama Mama

4 ounces pineapple juice
½ ounce dark rum
½ ounce Coco Lopez or coconut liqueur
¼ ounce rum
¼ ounce Kahlua
Juice of half a lemon
Maraschino cherry
Crushed ice

Pour liquid ingredients over ice and mix well. Garnish with cherry.

Frozen Sunrise Margarita

1 lime, cut in half
1 (6-ounce) can frozen orange juice concentrate,
    thawed
3 cups crushed ice
1 cup tequila
¼ cup powdered sugar
Granulated sugar

Using one half of the lime, rub the rims of four glasses, then dip the rims in granulated sugar. Set aside. Squeeze the juice from both lime halves into the blender, then add the remaining ingredients. Blend on high speed until smooth, then pour into the glasses. Serves four.

Golden Dream

½ ounce galliano
½ ounce crème de cacao
½ ounce triple sec
½ ounce orange juice
1½ ounces heavy cream
Crushed ice

Pour all ingredients over ice and mix well.

Long Island Iced Tea

½ ounce vodka
½ ounce gin
½ ounce light rum
½ ounce triple sec
¼ ounce tequila
1 tablespoon lemon juice
6 ounces Coke
Crushed ice
Lemon slice
Mint sprig

Pour liquors and lemon juice over ice and mix well. Add coke and garnish with the lemon slice and mint sprig.

Mimosa

3 ounces champagne, chilled
3 ounces orange juice
1 tablespoon Grand Marnier

Stir champagne and orange juice together in a wine glass, then top with Grand Marnier.

Northern Sunset

2 tablespoons Nestle's Quick (chocolate)
5 teaspoons instant coffee granules
1½ cups boiling water
1 tablespoon amaretto
1 tablespoon Kahlua
Whipped cream

Stir chocolate powder and instant coffee into the boiling water to dissolve, then stir in the amaretto and Kahlua. Pour into mugs and top with whipped cream. Serves two.

Orange Blossom

1 ounce gin
½ ounce triple sec
2 ounces orange juice
Crushed ice

Fill a mixing glass with ice, then add liquid ingredients. Shake well and strain into a chilled glass.

Sundowner

1½ ounces cognac
½ ounce galliano
½ ounce amaretto
1 tablespoon grenadine
Sweet and sour mix
Crushed ice

Pour cognac, galliano, and amaretto over ice and mix well. Fill with sweet and sour mix, and top with grenadine.

Sunlight Sipper

6 ounces pineapple juice, chilled
2 teaspoons peach schnapps
2 teaspoons light rum
2 teaspoons amaretto
Crushed ice

Pour all ingredients over ice and mix well.

Sunshine Cooler

3 scoops vanilla ice cream
1 ounce amaretto
Maraschino cherry

Blend ice cream and amaretto until smooth. Pour into glass and garnish with a cherry.

Tequila Sunrise

1½ ounces tequila
4 ounces orange juice
½ ounce grenadine
Crushed ice

Pour tequila and orange juice over ice and stir. Top with grenadine.

Bibliography

Andrassy, Stella. *The Solar Cookbook*. Dobbs Ferry, NY: Earth Books, a division of Morgan & Morgan Publishers, 1981.

Carroll, William. *Superstitions: 10,000 You Really Need*. San Marcos, CA: Coda Publications, 1988.

Cunningham, Scott. *The Complete Book of Oils, Incenses, and Brews*. St. Paul, MN: Llewellyn Publications, 1989.

———. *Cunningham's Encyclopedia of Crystal, Gem and Metal Magic*. St. Paul, MN: Llewellyn Publications, 1987.

———. *Cunningham's Encyclopedia of Magical Herbs*. St. Paul, MN: Llewellyn Publications, 1986.

Daniels, Estelle. *Astrological Magick*. York Beach, ME: Samuel Weiser, Inc., 1995.

David, Judithann H. *Michael's Gemstone Dictionary*. Channeled by J. P. Van Hulle. Orinda, CA: The Michael Educational Foundation and Affinity Press, 1986.

Drew, A. J. *Wicca For Men*. Secaucus, NJ: Carol Publishing Group, 1998.

Dues, Greg. *Catholic Customs and Traditions*. Mystic, CT: Twenty-Third Publications, 1992.

Eason, Cassandra. *A Practical Guide to Witchcraft and Magick Spells*. Berkshire, UK: Quantam, an imprint of W. Foulsham & Co. Ltd., 2001.

Flannery, Austin, O. P. *Vatican Council II: The Conciliar and Post Conciliar Documents*. Northport, NY: Costello Publishing Company, Inc., 1975.

Hope, Murry. *Practical Egyptian Magic*. New York: St. Martin's Press, 1984.

Kerenyi, Karl. *Goddesses of Sun and Moon*. Translated from German by Murray Stein. Dallas: Spring Publications, Inc., 1979.

Kingsbury, Stewart A., Mildred E. Kingsbury, and Wolfgang Mieder. *Weather Wisdom*. New York: Peter Lang Publishing, Inc., 1996.

Kunz, George Frederick. *The Curious Lore of Precious Stones*. Copyright 1913 by J. B. Lippincott Company, Philadelphia, PA. Copyright renewed 1941 by Ruby Kunz Zinsser; published 1971 by Dover Publications, Inc., New York, by special arrangement with J. P. Lippincott Company.

Malbrough, Ray T. *Charms, Spells & Formulas*. St. Paul, MN: Llewellyn Publications, 1986.

Medici, Marina. *Good Magic*. London: Mcmillan London Limited, 1988; New York: Prentice Hall Press, a Division of Simon & Schuster Inc., 1989.

Melody. *Love Is in the Earth: A Kaleidoscope of Crystals*. Wheat Ridge, CO: Earth-Love Publishing House, 1995.

Monaghan, Patricia. *The New Book of Goddesses and Heroines*. St. Paul, MN: Llewellyn Publications, 1997.

Morrison, Dorothy. *Bud, Blossom, & Leaf: The Magical Herb Gardener's Handbook*. St. Paul, MN: Llewellyn Publications, 2001.

———. *The Craft: A Witch's Book of Shadows*. St. Paul, MN: Llewellyn Publications, 2001.

———. *Everyday Magic: Spells and Rituals for Modern Living*. St. Paul, MN: Llewellyn Publications, 1998.

Riva, Anna. *The Modern Herbal Spellbook: The Magical Uses of Herbs*. Toluca Lake, CA: International Imports, 1974.

———. *The Secrets of Magical Seals*. Toluca Lake, CA: International Imports, 1975.

Slater, Herman. *The Magickal Formulary*. New York: Magickal Childe Inc., 1981.

Telesco, Patricia. *Magick Made Easy*. New York: HarperSan-Francisco, a division of Harper Collins Publishers, 1999.

———. *Spinning Spells, Weaving Wonders*. Freedom, CA: Crossing Press, 1996.

Watterson, Barbara. *Ancient Egypt*. Gloucester, UK: Sutton Publishing Ltd., 1998.

Index